Academic Libraries in Greece
The Present Situation and Future Prospects

Academic Libraries in Greece
The Present Situation and Future Prospects

Dean H. Keller, MLS
Editor

Routledge
Taylor & Francis Group
New York   London

First published by

The Haworth Press, Inc., 10 Alice Street, Binghamton, NY 13904-1580

This edition published 2013 by Routledge

Routledge   Routledge
Taylor & Francis Group   Taylor & Francis Group
711 Third Avenue   2 Park Square, Milton Park
New York, NY 10017   Abingdon, Oxon OX14 4RN

Routledge is an imprint of the Taylor & Francis Group, an informa business

Library of Congress Cataloging-in-Publication Data

Academic libraries in Greece : the present situation and future prospects / Dean H. Keller, editor.
    p.   cm.
    Includes bibliographical references and index.
    ISBN 1-56024-365-1
    1. Libraries, University and college–Greece. I. Keller, Dean H.
Z675.U5A337   1993
027.7′09495–dc20   92-22836
                                                                 CIP

To Tom and Gina Davis

CONTENTS

ABOUT THE EDITOR

Dean H. Keller, MLS, spent six months as an exchange librarian at Aristotle University in Thessaloniki, Greece, in 1989. Currently, he is Associate Dean of Libraries and Professor of Library Administration at Kent State University in Ohio, where he has worked since 1958. A member of the Bibliographical Society of America and The Manuscript Society, Mr. Keller is the author of several books and articles in the fields of librarianship, bibliography, rare books, history, and English and American Literature.

Contributors

Nicolaos Alexandrou is Professor of Chemistry and Chair of the Library Committee at Aristotle University in Thessaloniki, Greece.

Nancy Birk is Associate Curator of Special Collections at the Kent State University Libraries, Kent, Ohio.

George D. Bokos is Head of the Department of Cataloging, National Library of Greece in Athens.

Thomas M. Davis is Professor of English and Coordinator of the Greek Exchange Program at Kent State University, Kent, Ohio.

Dimitrios Dimitriou is Director of the Central Library of Aristotle University in Thessaloniki, Greece.

Peter D. Haikalis is a member of the faculty of the J. Paul Leonard Library at San Francisco State University in California.

Dimitris Karageorgiou is a doctoral candidate in Educational Administration at Kent State University, Kent, Ohio.

Stella Korobili is Professor in the School of Library Science at the Technical Education Institute of Thessaloniki, Greece.

Michael Kreyche is Head of Systems at the Kent State University Libraries, Kent, Ohio.

James Krikelas is Professor of Library Science at the University of Wisconsin in Madison.

Martha Kyrillidou is a doctoral student in the School of Library and Information Science at the University of Illinois.

Mersini Moreleli-Cacouris is Director of the School of Library Science at the Technical Education Institute of Thessaloniki, Greece.

Alex Noel-Tod is Senior Assistant Librarian, University of East Anglia, Norwich, England.

Athena Salaba is a member of the staff of the Central Library of Aristotle University in Thessaloniki, Greece.

Vicki Syroglou-Bouki is Librarian at the American Center in Thessaloniki, Greece.

Don L. Tolliver is Dean of Libraries and Media Services at Kent State University, Kent, Ohio.

Michael Tzekakis is Director of the Library at the University of Crete in Rethymno, Greece.

Introduction

Dean H. Keller

The purpose of this collection of essays is to focus attention on academic libraries in Greece at a time when the potential for changes and advances in librarianship in the country is great. More professionally and technically trained Greek librarians are available; contact with American, British, and European librarians is widespread; new technology is becoming more readily available; and the influence of the European Economic Community is beginning to be felt.

The authors of the papers that follow hold a wide variety of library or library education positions in Greece, England, and the United States, or they are closely connected with higher education and libraries. Each brings unique sets of training, experience, and points of view to the topics they discuss. While many subjects are treated, it is obvious that there is much more to be said about the academic library situation in Greece. The reader will find, however, that the essays included here describe major trends and suggest future directions, and they are believed to be representative of what is happening in Greek academic librarianship today.

It should not be surprising that three of the essays–by George D. Bokos, Michael Kreyche, and James Krikelas and Michael Tzekakis–deal with automation; the subject is touched upon in other essays as well. Expectations are high that automation will stimulate advances in all areas of librarianship in Greece. James Krikelas in 1984 and Nancy Birk and Dimitris Karageorgiou in 1988 published general surveys of Greek academic libraries and these papers are reprinted in this collection. They are the only previously published papers to be included.

Mersini Moreleli-Cacouris has provided an historical account of library education in Greece, along with a description of the current library science program at the Technical Education Institute in Thessaloniki. Stella Korobili discusses issues of collection development and interlibrary loan. Libraries such as those maintained by the American Center and British Council indirectly support the work of students of English and American literature, history, and culture at the universities. Vicki Syroglou-Bouki, the librarian of the American Center in Thessaloniki, has provided a description of the Center's collection, services, and facilities.

Peter D. Haikalis has described the Library at the University of Crete in Rethymno, and additional information about that library will be found in the above-mentioned article by James Krikelas and Michael Tzekakis. Nicolaos Alexandrou and Dimitrios Dimitriou have provided a description of the Central Library of Aristotle University in Thessaloniki. Martha Kyrillidou and Alex Noel-Tod pay special, detailed attention to the English Department Library at Aristotle University.

In 1984, Kent State University established an exchange program with Aristotle University, and, almost from the beginning, the University Libraries became a part of that program. Thomas M. Davis has described the exchange with emphasis on the role the Libraries have played in it. One of the Greek librarians who participated in the exchange, Athena Salaba, has provided a chronicle of her experiences. Finally, Don L. Tolliver, Dean of Libraries and Media Services at Kent State University has made some general philosophical observations on the value of international library cooperation, especially in regard to Greece.

It remains for me to acknowledge and thank all those who made this collection possible. First, of course, I am indebted to all those who contributed essays to this collection, and to Michael Kreyche and Athena Salaba for translations. Without them, there would be no book. I am grateful to Peter Gellatly of the Haworth Press for his interest in this project and for his encouragement to carry it out. The publishers of *International Library Review* and *Libri* generously gave permission to reprint articles by James Krikelas, Nancy Birk, and Dimitris Karageorgiou. Kent State University's Office of Research and Sponsored Programs also provided support for the typing of the final manuscript. Thanks to all.

International Interlibrary Cooperation: Exchanging Goals, Values, and Culture

Don L. Tolliver

In our formal education for librarianship, the MLS provides little opportunity for us to gain even a minimal understanding of academic librarianship worldwide. We may hear a guest speaker from this country who has spent some time in libraries in another culture. We may get anecdotal comments from professors who have traveled internationally. They make casual comments about other cultures, and perhaps they may informally discuss their impressions of library facilities, collections, or services in the countries they have visited. We may read occasional articles in the professional journals about libraries in other countries.

Likewise, the experiences we typically gain in U.S. academic libraries provide few opportunities for exposure to our library colleagues in other cultural settings. While we know that cultures of countries differ, we may not always realize that the fundamental purposes, roles, and philosophies of higher education in those countries are likely to be quite diverse as well. Professional library conferences and meetings sponsored in the U.S. seldom focus on the issues, priorities, or concerns of those librarians working in academic settings outside of this country. Even the differences between Canadian academic library environments and those in the U.S. could not be well articulated by most academic librarians in the States, though some of these differences are not as subtle as one might think.

WHAT WE HAVE TO OFFER

Given these minimal levels of understanding, it is surprising how often we in the U.S. academic libraries are asked to interact with our international colleagues. Perhaps much of our success in these international interactions, whether they be formal or informal exchange programs, must be credited to our colleagues' better understanding of our culture than to our knowledge of theirs. Further, the U.S. has maintained leadership in most areas of higher education. Several examples come quickly to mind. A remarkable number of public and private institutions of higher education are available for students in the U.S. Most of these institutions enjoy an adequate to relatively strong level of funding. Taken together, the public and private institutions provide numerous avenues of access to higher education for U.S. high school graduates. Students in the U.S. are exposed to a fairly high standard of quality instruction in most higher education environments, and our system of higher education strongly promotes the furtherance of knowledge through systematic research in increasingly diverse fields. One spin-off of this emphasis on research in higher education in the U.S. has been the emergence of many academic research libraries with strong collections and much experience in the development and implementation of technological systems. These systems can identify and retrieve relevant information from sources located in other national or international library and scholarly settings, as well as local material and information.

Thus, our emphasis on, and support of, higher education in the U.S., when compared with most countries, naturally generates strong international interest in what we have accomplished. This has been especially true since the late 1950s, when many academic developments took place following renewed support for science education. Such developments during the past 30 years have included advances in library and information methodologies as well. Even though we may be quite ill-equipped to interact by using other languages–or have a poor understanding of, and sensitivity to, other cultures–we are, nevertheless, in a position to bring strong support, both philosophically and technically, to library programs in these other cultural settings.

WHAT WE HAVE TO GAIN

We, too, have an opportunity to learn much in such interchanges. First and foremost, we begin to recognize that there is more than one way to approach academic issues and library problems. Second, we begin to reflect on our own environment back in the U.S. When we do so, we may note that bureaucracy is bureaucracy, and while theirs may not work for us, it seems to work for them. The degree of effectiveness of any bureaucracy will remain a subject of conjecture. After exposure to other bureaucracies, we may better appreciate the spirit of self-determination and the degree of financial support most U.S. academic institutions enjoy. In turn, U.S. academic libraries are relatively well financed and typically receive strong political support from academic colleagues. Let us hope we begin to realize the opportunities and flexibility our support base provides to encourage advances in academic librarianship. Further, as we begin to understand our international colleagues' commitment to change and modernization of library applications, we sense that they often might exceed us if they were presented with similar opportunities and strong governmental and political support.

Perhaps an example is in order. During the 1980s in the United Kingdom, the Thatcher government enlisted the University Grants Council (UGC) to set priorities for higher education. Control of university development and change became highly centralized, which naturally led to considerable tension within the university environments. This radical response from the Thatcher government addressed the belief that higher education had been "over built" and that duplicate academic programs were no longer affordable. While centralized downsizing of higher education in the U.K. may have made it more efficient, did this make it more effective? It certainly became less accessible to students. Perhaps in the long term, the more important victim of centralized control was the loss of local control of priorities and utilization of faculty creativity. Without self-determination, advances in creative thought that would enhance both instructional and research efforts may be slowed substantially. One wonders how advances in academe would have fared if incentives for change had rested with each U.K. institution of higher education.

THE KENT STATE/ARISTOTLE EXCHANGE

The Kent State University Libraries have become an important part of the formal exchange between Kent State University and

Aristotle University in Thessaloniki, Greece. Since 1985, five librarians from Kent have participated for a full nine semesters in various capacities within the Libraries of Aristotle University. Kent Library staff have been involved in the physical reorganization of collections and cataloging of the English Department Library. They have concerned themselves with issues of collection development, acquisition policies and systems, library instruction, automation, coordination between and across departmental libraries, and definition of the role of the central library. During the more recent stages of our exchange, we have worked to achieve library cooperation across institutions of higher education, with a primary focus on cooperative library automation development and implementation. Also, staff from the Central Library and departmental libraries of Aristotle University have participated in practicum experiences within the Kent State University Libraries. Some have enrolled in, and graduated from, Kent's School of Library and Information Science.

In spite of wide differences in culture, and especially the differences in university cultures, I believe this exchange has so far had a profound and positive effect on both universities. At Kent I see a better appreciation of the position of libraries within U.S. academic settings. We recognize that much hard work has gone before us and that our position within the academic environment permits us to recommend and set policy and procedures that maximize our personnel, facilities, and acquisition efforts to further library service and systematically improve collections and access methods.

Academic librarians in U.S. institutions of higher education are typically viewed as full professional partners by discipline-oriented faculty. Without the expertise of librarians, who over the decades have developed and maintained well-organized library service and collections, the productivity of most academic departments would not be at present levels. Advances in research and the generation of new knowledge in the U.S. would be slowed markedly without these information professionals. Today, U.S. scholars require not only strong, well-organized collections held locally but also access to information and collections found in other libraries or distant laboratories. Such access to support major research efforts (e.g., disease control, global warming, etc.) implies organized professional library support, interdisciplinary study, and cooperation based on a natural sharing of information. This points to the necessity of the library as a full academic, instructional, and research partner. This necessity is only now beginning to be recognized in the culture of Greek higher education.

Thus, much of our work in Greece–and with Greek library staff who work with us in the Libraries at Kent State University–centers on issues that impact the culture of higher education as it is practiced at Aristotle University. While the effects of our efforts to date have not been sweeping, they have, nevertheless, been significant. Questions are being raised by faculty in some quarters of Aristotle University about the lack of professionally prepared librarians. The need to expand library education beyond the technical schools may soon be voiced. The importance of leadership to improve library organization, cataloging, acquisitions, bibliographic instruction, technological applications, reference, and other services is not recognized by several university faculty leaders. A few are even beginning to press for more library cooperative efforts across universities. In the following areas, we have witnessed several positive changes regarding how libraries are formed, managed, and supported at Aristotle University: (1) collecting journals and arranging them alphabetically by title and chronologically within a departmental library; (2) politically charged issues of staffing, professional staffing, and an identification of the role of librarians in the academic process; and (3) the beginnings of cooperative library automation development between Aristotle University and the University of Crete. We have also witnessed changes in ourselves, often noting our inadequacies and faculty assumptions about "what's best" for this or that library issue in Greece.

To be truly successful, we must maintain open minds and work to achieve a true exchange of ideas, since the policies, practices, and technologies we bring from the U.S. can never be imposed on others. They must be introduced cautiously and with respect. Those who have participated in the exchange between the two universities have been influenced significantly by their exchange experiences and have often returned to become more reflective and valued staff in their home libraries.

Academic Libraries in Greece

James Krikelas

External experts visiting Greece to consult on library development have been hampered until recently by the paucity of published
information. In the past few years, a number of English language
articles have appeared covering a variety of subjects and libraries;
but missing from the literature is any extensive treatment of academic libraries.[1] As part of a senior Fulbright Lectureship, I had the
opportunity to spend some time studying the situation at one of the
largest universities in Greece. I also got to visit a number of other
institutions of higher education.[2] This report, therefore, is a summa-
tion of some *impressions* gained through such visits.

As with all other nations, the specific character of Greece has had
a pronounced influence on the development and growth of libraries.
Although it is difficult to describe the nature of this character fully
within the limits of this paper, it is important to realize that geographic and historical factors have interacted to produce a cultural
environment that may be very unfamiliar to visitors from any other
country.[3]

BACKGROUND

Greece is a small nation of just over nine million people occupy-
ing a region of 132,000 square kilometers (50,950 square miles). It
is located on one of the three major European peninsulas that reach
southward into the Mediterranean Sea. Located at the eastern end of
that sea, it has been–and continues to be–a crossroads between

---

This article was first published in *International Library Review*, 16, 1984.

Western European and Near East Asia. Thus, in many ways, it is more similar in customs, habits, and attitudes to its eastern non-European neighbors than to its seabound and distant neighbor to the west (Italy). On the other hand, it shares many traits with Slavic countries to the north–a commonality in its historic efforts to achieve political independence from Ottoman rule and (with the exception of Albania, which retained an Islamic majority) in its having a common, albeit diverse, religion (Eastern Orthodoxy). Frequently grouped with these Slavic neighbors as a Balkan country, it is also less Balkan than they are, as one American analyst has noted:

> Although in some respects Greece was closely tied to its northern neighbors . . . [Yugoslavia, Albania, and Bulgaria] . . . it should be considered a Mediterranean rather than a Balkan country. Its long indented coastline, together with the relative poverty of its resources, led its people to seek their fortunes in shipping, and made them leaders in the Mediterranean carrying trade.[4]

Historically, Greece traces its roots as a nation back over two thousand years. But in reality, the modern nation of Greece was born only 150 years ago, achieving independence from Ottoman rule in the nineteenth century (1832) and acquiring almost a quarter of its current territory as recently as 1913. Much of this history has been marked by political instability and devastating wars both international and civil. The result is a nation of contrasting social, economic, and political styles that frequently bewilder foreigners. It is within this unusual environment (neither Occidental nor Oriental) that one must view academic library development.

GREEK UNIVERSITIES

Greek universities are, as in other countries, the capstone of the educational system. Under Ottoman rule, the Greek Orthodox Church played a dominant role in the education of Greeks, and its influence continues. After independence, however, Greece installed a three-tiered educational system that contained aspects of French elementary and Bavarian secondary education.[5] The establishment of a university in Athens in 1847 provided the third tier–higher education. During the succeeding 145 years, all levels of education have undergone growth and extensive revision. Today, the national system of education offers various types of instruction. Post-secondary education is provided through four categories of institutions: university-level; higher schools of teacher education; vocational teacher-training schools; and centers for higher and professional technical studies. Of these four types, only the university-level schools are considered in this paper. This group can be subdivided into two parts: (1) schools that are true multi-faculty universities (the *panepistimia*) and (2) other university-level schools (*anotates scholés*), which are characterized by their focus on a single area of study.

The universities are of relatively recent origin; the school in Athens (founded in 1847) and the one in Thessaloniki (established in 1925) are the oldest and the largest. The University of Patras and the University of Ioannina were created by law in 1964; the University of Thrace and the University of Crete were founded in 1973. Each of the latter two schools has a divided campus (that is, faculties are located in separate cities). Among the eight university-level institutions, two can trace their roots to the nineteenth century, but neither reached university status until this century–the National Metsovian Polytechnic in 1914 and the School of Fine Arts in 1930.[6] Both are located in Athens, as are the Panteios School of Political Science, the Agricultural School, and the School of Economics and Commercial Science. The other university-level schools are located in Thessaloniki (industrial studies), Piraeus (industrial studies), and Irakleon (site of the newly created polytechnic).

Statistical information, admittedly of questionable accuracy, is useful for illustrating the relative size of these fourteen units (see Table 1). Although each institution has its own character, certain factors become evident as one travels to various academic libraries in Greece. Since I gained the closest familiarity with the University of Thessaloniki, I find it convenient to use it as a basis for making comparisons and for identifying major issues.

TABLE 1. Greek Universities

School	Students*	Teaching staff*	Library volumes+
University of			
Athens	43,013	2,089	403,000
Thessaloniki	31,074	2,101	800,000
Patras	4,199	291	7,000
Ioannina	3,422	242	110,000
Thrace	1,245	134	56,000
Crete	n.a.	n.a.	n.a.
School of Economics and			
Commercial Science	8,362	129	30,000
School of Industrial Studies			
(Piraeus)	7,531	91	8,000
School of Industrial Studies			
(Thessaloniki)	6,456	66	10,000
Panteios School of Political			
Science	6,606	145	50,000
National Polytechnic	5,735	673	150,000
School of Agriculture	894	155	6,000
School of Fine Arts	307	31	11,000
Polytechnic of Crete	n.a.	n.a.	n.a.

n.a. = not available
Sources: *Massialas[7] and + Kokkinis[8]

THE ARISTOTELEAN UNIVERSITY
OF THESSALONIKI

The Aristotelean University of Thessaloniki is located on a large, 100-acre campus in the center of Greece's second-largest city. Among its many buildings is a separate, central library that was constructed over a ten-year period and occupied in 1974. The building is unique in Greece, since it is currently the only academic structure designed exclusively for use as a library. The university in Athens (the National and Kapodistrean University of Athens) technically shares the facilities of the National Library but in reality does not have a central library.

The library building in Thessaloniki is partitioned into separate units comprising the main library, a student study hall containing a textbook reading collection, and the ubiquitous snack shop. Inspection of the holdings, however, reveals that the central library is the repository of only a small portion of the million volumes that the University is said to own.[9] An on-site study conducted in October and November 1980 revealed that approximately 200 quasi-autonomous libraries were active in ordering and acquiring materials during the previous academic year. It is in these units that much of the University's book collection resides, with some collections reaching 25,000 volumes in size.

Collection Development

Dispersion of the collection is not unusual among academic libraries in Greece. Even where central libraries exist–which is the case with most of the smaller institutions–the pattern of decentralization persists. There are at least two major causes of collection dispersion–physical limitations and a tradition fostered by the educational practices in the county. Physical limits are the result of a lack of facilities as well as the decision to share the University among several communities. The Democrates University of Thrace, for example, has two campuses: one in Komotini for the law school and one in Xanthi for engineering. (A third campus, for the proposed medical school, may be situated in Alexandroupolis.) The campus in Komotini is the site of a former secondary school complex and consists of a few interconnected buildings. Since the facilities are too small to accommodate all departments of the law school, other quarters a few kilometers from the main structure have been occupied. The off-campus departments have already begun to develop their own collections at the second location–independent of the main library–and at least two separate libraries now exist at the second site. Similarly, at Xanthi, where the campus is a single four-story building, there was pressure to extract the mathematics collection and to house the materials nearer to the faculty offices.

In other schools, it is not unusual to find much of the collection on "permanent loan" to the faculty. The trend has reached an extreme in Ioannina, where the library administrative office, situated in a downtown building some distance from the campus, acts only as a central acquisitions and listing service–one can hardly call it cataloging–that disperses the ordered materials to individual faculty libraries. A large reading room exists, but not a centralized collection. And in Athens, the growth of the University has led to the relocation of some departments (and their libraries) to two suburban sites that are remote from the downtown campus. The result is that 87 identifiable collections[10] are even more dispersed.

The second factor that is partially responsible for collection dispersion is related to a long tradition in the educational system. Having borrowed its university model from nineteenth-century Europe, Greece has been slow in instituting major changes, partly because the system satisfies perceived national needs and partly because vested interests have developed and it is difficult to eliminate them. In Thessaloniki, for example, the University is organized into nine schools or faculties. One, the School of Philosophy, has an Institute for Foreign Languages and Philology attached to it, and this has resulted in ten large faculty units. Each unit is subdivided into "chairs" that represent the various subject components making up the broader discipline. These chairs are roughly equivalent to academic departments in the United States, except that they tend to be more narrow in subject scope and smaller in size.

The chair is occupied by a professor (*kathegetes*), who may have an indefinite (lifetime) appointment or a shorter, specified term. Associated with most professors are auxiliary teaching positions (*epimeletes* and *voithe*) that are frequently grouped to form a larger unit known as a clinic, laboratory, or seminar–depending on the subject matter. The 1980-81 University catalog lists 305 professorships at various levels of tenure and approximately 315 individual chairs, clinics, laboratories, and seminars (indicating vacancies or that some professors hold more than one appointment). All academic and, hence, administrative power resides in these chairs. Frequently, this power is exercised in the interest of the smaller unit rather than for the common (university) good.

While the number of professorships differs from university to university, there is almost no variation in the practice of collection development. Authority for selection of material rests with the faculty. This authority is underscored by the fact that the budget for such materials is controlled by the professor and not by the library. Thus, what may appear to be a library budget is actually a combined budget for the various chair libraries, with some additional funds set aside for the main library, where one exists. That this situation prevails seems reasonable to Greek professors, for they are the principal users of the books and journals. Student interest in, and access to, library materials is limited. Because of a conservative education tradition in Greece, there is a heavy dependence on annual examinations as the method for determining course grades; the examination places primary emphasis on rote recital (or complete recall) of accepted interpretations of the discipline under examination. Little value is placed on independent study or research, and students do not regularly utilize non-textbook materials. There are, of course, individual exceptions to this pattern, but it is sufficiently common to raise some questions among students and faculty about the relevance of free access to materials other than required texts and a few study aids. Nevertheless, even this limited need for materials is hampered by uncontrolled dispersion of the collection.

The presence or absence of a central library or collection is not the major issue. The basic question is whether the needs of the academic community are adequately met by the service provided. If they are, then change simply to bring Greek academic libraries into conformity with Western standards is unwarranted. One of the consequences of faculty control, however, is unintentional duplication of materials and efforts. And, in fact, this condition was observed not only among libraries at Thessaloniki but at other campuses as well. The result is that collection development for the university (or *anotati schole*) is uncoordinated and represents a wasteful use of scarce economic resources. Then why does the practice persist? The answer is not difficult to find, and it is not unlike the situation common among European and American libraries in the nineteenth century. Carl White's commentary on this topic is especially pertinent:

The seminar library resembles, in convenience, organization, use of space and how it is controlled, a personal library, and some scholars remain strongly attached to it for precisely this reason. It is the model they are accustomed to and like. But while the seminar library, along with libraries which are organized and administered along similar lines, still survives and flourishes, no major country accepts it any longer as the best model to use when planning further library advances. There are several reasons why it is being superseded, but they add up to saying that it is giving ground to the same forces which pushed aside the once all-sufficient personal library. . . . There are more fields [of study], with more overlapping interests, as well as more publication in each one. . . . The seminar library is designed best to serve the private interests of a small group, whereas we now live in a day when library service must, in fairness to all scholars and all taxpayers, be planned to serve the greatest good of the greatest number at minimum cost.[11]

Greek academic libraries seem to be at the threshold of change. An increasing number of Greek professors travel abroad to study, and they return with different ideas about the educational process and the role of the library. Furthermore, as the number of universities and "higher schools" has grown, it becomes apparent that extensive duplication of resources within, as well as between, campuses is a luxury that can be afforded no longer. Nevertheless, it is difficult to make drastic changes without creating strong resistance. The plan to create a single, centralized library at Thessaloniki, and the resulting failure to coordinate the collection development efforts, offers some evidence that change will come slowly. One solution at that institution might be to develop school-wide libraries, but again, lack of physical space in existing structures mitigates against speedy achievement of that objective.

Bibliographic Organization

If collection unification is not currently feasible, at least some of the access difficulties could be alleviated by creating a union catalog for each campus. And, in fact, the central library of the University of Thessaloniki has attempted to maintain some record of the materials acquired. In a rather unusual procedure, the library receives information about book purchases without actually participating in the selection or acquisitions (ordering) process. In time (and this may vary from a few weeks to a number of years), the library receives from the various departmental collections the books that have been purchased, whereupon the library staff catalogs and classifies them (using one of the 200 classification schemes devised by the departmental chairs) and then returns the books to the appropriate faculty library. For a number of years, the central library was able to produce a limited card set for each book. Usually, the set consisted of an author, title, a "catchword" subject entry, and a shelflist card for the appropriate faculty collection. Sometime in the mid-1970s, the limited amount of clerical assistance was further decreased to the point where typed cards could no longer be produced without creating an intolerable backlog of books. Instead, a new procedure was implemented whereby the cataloger's handwritten workslip was photocopied and used to create a "temporary" single-access listing as a supplement to the card catalog. As pressure to get the books back to the faculty more quickly continued to grow, even this step was deleted; by 1980, only a cataloger's workslip was being created. This was filed, by class number, in another "temporary" catalog, this time housed in one of the four separate cataloging sections and thus not available to the general patron. For all practical purposes, therefore, a full catalog of holdings no longer exists. The situation is the same at Athens, where collection development coordination is nonexistent.

Even in the smaller schools, a true union catalog of holdings is not always possible. At Ioannina, for example, a single record is created for each acquisition, but the card is filed alphabetically by author in the central catalog. In this catalog, cards are kept separate for each faculty collection, thus producing a series of departmental listings rather than a union catalog for the University. The two campuses of the University of Thrace have separate catalogs, and no effort is made to share either bibliographic records or resources. Even the implementation of a computer-based card-catalog production system[12] has not resulted in a catalog, only in a backlog. The printed cards have not been interfiled because there is not enough staff to type in the accession number on the card set. As of March 1981, the cards were used for circulation control rather than to create a catalog.

Cataloging backlogs are common because so much of the work consists of original (rather than copy) cataloging; there is no national bibliography. In the absence of an adequate catalog, some books may receive the same expensive original cataloging attention a second and third time. Additional effort must be devoted to the creation and revision of various classification schemes. Some libraries have abandoned the attempt to maintain their own schedules and have instead adopted versions of the Dewey Decimal Classification (DDC) or Universal Decimal Classification (UDC) System. To achieve some conformity, the Library of Congress Classification (LCC) was put in place at Thessaloniki, but it is unsatisfactory–as are other schedules–because of its weaknesses in dealing with various aspects of Greek history, geography, religion, and modern literature. The need to deal with materials in a variety of foreign languages adds yet another obstacle.

The libraries at the University of Thessaloniki add approximately 20,000 volumes a year (over the past five years). It has been estimated by the main library staff that almost 85 percent of these purchases are foreign titles. A study of the 1979 invoices supported this contention. Of the 17,391 titles purchased by the faculty libraries, 2,080 of them (11.96 percent) were in Greek. The actual distribution of foreign titles, of course, varies greatly with the subject matter, and in some cases (for example, the School of Theology and the School of Philosophy), the number of Greek titles runs as high as one-third of all purchases. On the other hand, purchases in other areas (such as math-physics, medicine, and, of course, foreign languages) are almost exclusively foreign titles. Further verification of this situation was obtained as part of an experimental project to implement a revised style of processing. Of a sample of 710 titles processed in a three-week period in late April and early May (1981), less than 6 percent were in Greek (see Table II).

The problem is complicated further because of the need to deal with a Greek and a Roman alphabet. In many libraries, the Roman sequence has been selected and Greek words are interfiled by their Roman equivalent. Thus, the Greek *omega*–the last letter of the Greek alphabet–is found among the Roman *ohs* (the fifteenth of twenty-six letters!). An alternative solution–used at the National Library and for the newest catalog at Thessaloniki–is to create two separate catalogs: one for Greek language materials and a second for non-Greek entries. Even this practice has required some decisions for dealing with other non-Roman foreign literatures (such as

TABLE 2. Language Distribution (n = 710 titles)

Language	Number	Percent
Greek	38	5.35
Foreign	672	94.65
Spanish	10	1.41
Italian	88	12.39
German	97	13.66
French	107	15.07
English	370	52.11

Russian). At Thessaloniki, all non-Roman foreign materials are cataloged by transliterating bibliographic information into English in order to facilitate using records created by the Library of Congress and the British National Bibliography. Such technical problems highlight the uncommon difficulties Greek librarians must deal with on a regular basis. At the same time, they must work within a system that places little value on their efforts, because of the currently low level of academic library use.

Library Personnel

The situation at Thessaloniki is illustrative of one of the major problems faced by all academic libraries in Greece. Staff on almost all campuses work under various constraints, not the least of which is the dearth of trained librarians. Problems in employing appropriate personnel for academic libraries are related to the interconnected factors of (1) the absence of an adequate program of education for librarianship in Greece and (2) the peculiar staffing practices in the country. In many ways, library positions are perceived as being interchangeable with clerical and administrative positions throughout the bureaucracy. Individuals may be transferred from one office to another because it is believed that no special training is necessary in such positions. Both factors reflect a general attitude that libraries are designed to do no more than acquire and store books and periodicals; there is very little understanding of library services beyond those functions.

The result is that library personnel find themselves having to perform tasks for which they have had no specific training. The obstacles to professional education are complex, and prospects for drastic changes seem unlikely.[13] On-the-job instruction is also frequently limited because many libraries have professors in the role of librarian. Even at Thessaloniki, where there is a director (librarian) for the main library, authority over departmental personnel is retained by the individual faculty member. Cumulatively, these departmental assistants outnumber the main library's staff. In mid-1980, the University library staff consisted of twenty-eight staff members (a number that includes three assistants for monitoring the textbook reading room), two bookstack pages, and two bindery clerks. The only typist in the library served as secretary to the director. Much smaller staffs were found on other campuses, none with more than six individuals in the main library or central administrative office. The situation might not be so desperate if traditional bibliographic aids were available to assist the staff. Unfortunately, only the most meager assistance is available. Various efforts have been made in recent years to rectify this situation, but only modest progress has been achieved.[14]

Changes in academic libraries are most likely to come only after changes in the general structure of Greek higher education. It would be tempting to export Western-style academic librarianship to the country, but the particular needs of Greece are best determined from within. The responsibility of visiting consultants is to apprise Greek librarians of the options available; to do so meaningfully requires some understanding of the current situation. This paper seeks to add to that understanding.

REFERENCE NOTES

1. As a convenience to the reader, a short bibliography of recently published articles on Greek libraries is appended.

2. Partial research support was provided through a grant from the Research Committee of the Graduate School of the University of Wisconsin-Madison. In addition to visits to various libraries in Thessaloniki, trips were made to the University of Thrace (Komotini and Xanthi campuses), the Universities of Patras and Ioannina, different departments at the University of Athens, as well as to the Polytechnic, the Panteios School of Political Science, the National Library, the Parliamentary Library, and various special libraries in Athens.

3. The reader may find two short books of particular interest in understanding modern Greece. They are: Richard Clogg, *A Short History of Modern Greece* (Cambridge: Cambridge University Press, 1979) and Douglas Dakin, *The Greek Struggle for Independence, 1821-1833* (London: B.T. Batsford, 1973).
4. Robert Lee Wolf, *The Balkans in Our Time* (Cambridge, Mass.: Harvard University Press, 1956), p. 8.
5. Byron G. Massialas, *The Educational System of Greece* (Washington: U.S. Department of Education, 1981), p. 1.
6. Ibid., p. 12.
7. Ibid., p. 12.
8. Spiro Kokkinis, "Bibliothikes Anotaton Ekpaideytikov Idrymatov Stin Ellada," *Diabazo* (Martios, 1980): s48.
9. This figure differs from the one reported by Kokkinis (see Table I). It is, however, the more frequently given number in most official reports, and it is the figure used by the library staff.
10. Kokkinis, p. 48.
11. Carl M. White. "Comparative Study of Library Systems," in *Bases of Modern Librarianship; a Study of Library Theory and Practice in Britain, Canada, Denmark, The Federal Republic of Germany and the United States*, ed. Carl M. White (Oxford: Pergamon Press, 1964), p. 14.
12. Pericles Papadoperakis, "The Automation Project at Library B of Thrace University," *Program*, 16 (April 1982): 57-66.
13. James Krikelas, "Education for Librarianship in Greece," *Library Quarterly* 52 (July 1982): 227-239.
14. For an overview of some of the existing tools, see the following: Anne Holmes, "Traps for Young Players: Some Comments on Purchasing Greek Material," *Australian Library Journal* 30, (November 1981): 124-128.

LIBRARIES AND LIBRARY RESOURCES OF GREECE: A SELECTED ENGLISH-LANGUAGE BIBLIOGRAPHY, 1973-1982

Cacouris, George M. 1973. "Libraries in Greece." *Encyclopedia of Library and Information Science*. New York: Marcel Dekker, vol. 10, pp. 180-190.
Cacouris, George M. 1973. "Library Education in Greece." *Encyclopedia of Library and Information Science*. New York: Marcel Dekker, vol. 10, pp. 190-195.
Demopoulos, J. 1982. "The History of the National Library of Greece." *International Library Review*, October, pp. 411-416.
Holmes, Anne. 1981. "Traps for Young Players: Some Comments on Purchasing Greek Material." *Australian Library Journal*, November, pp. 124-128.
Krikelas, James. 1982. "Education for Librarianship in Greece." *Library Quarterly*, July, pp. 227-239.
Moffat, Edward S. 1980. "Leading the Greek Library Association." *Leads*, Spring, pp. 1-2.

Palamiotou, Sophie. 1979. "Greek Libraries: Problems, Proposals." *Leads*, Summer, pp. 1-3.

Panagiotou, Evlambia. 1973. "University Library Buildings: A View from Greece." *New Library World*, April, pp. 81-82.

Papadoperakis, Pericles. 1982. "The Automation Project at Library B of Thrace University." *Program*, April, pp. 57-66.

Placotari, Alexandra. 1974. "Literature for Children in Greece." *Bookbird*, Number 3, pp. 37-43.

Ratliff, Neil. 1979. "Resources for Music Research in Greece-An Overview." *Notes: The Quarterly Journal of the Music Library Association*, September, pp. 50-64.

Rhodes, Dennis E. 1980. *Incunabula in Greece: A First Census*. Munchen: Kraus International Publications.

St. Clair, Guy. 1982. "Visiting Special Libraries in Greece: A Few Surprises for the Western Librarian." *Special Libraries*, July, pp. 202-206.

Thanopoulou, K. 1980. "Greece." *ALA World Encyclopedia of Library and Information Services*, Chicago: American Library Association, pp. 223-224.

Academic Libraries in Greece: A New Profile

Nancy Birk
Dimitris Karageorgiou

Although Greece is often placed in the context of the birthplace of Western education, its university-level schools of formal education are a fairly recent development. The University of Athens was the first to be founded in (1837), followed by the University of Thessaloniki in 1925. Since then, the university system has expanded to include seven more: the Universities of Patra, Ioannina, Thraki, Kriti, Thessalia, the Aigaio, and the Ionio.

At the university level are another eight professional schools, each specializing in one area of study: (1) School of Economics and Commercial Science-Athens; (2) School of Industrial Studies-Pireas; (3) School of Industrial Studies-Thessaloniki; (4) Panteios School of Political Science-Athens; (5) National Polytechnic-Athens; (6) School of Agriculture-Athens; (7) School of Fine Arts-Athens; and (8) Polytechnic-Kriti. There are private schools as well, but they are foreign institutions and not at university level, though they have the name "college" as part of their title (e.g., Anatolia College in Thessaloniki and Athens College in Athens). All these higher-level institutions include libraries of one form or another.

James Krikelas, in his article "Academic Libraries in Greece,"[1] clearly outlines academic library development. The political climate has changed since that publication, and different library issues have evolved. This article seeks to expand and update Krikelas' foundational work by: describing the various library systems of the university-level institutions; providing information on the legal framework within which they exist; and analyzing and pondering the issues and characteristics unique to the Greek library situation.

This article was first published in *Libri*, 38, 1988.

THE GREEK EDUCATIONAL SYSTEM

An overview of the Greek educational system is essential to an understanding of the context in which academic libraries exist and of their role within Greek higher education and cultural society. The Greek educational system consists of four levels:

1. Primary: *Primary school* starting at the age of five, for a duration of six years.
2. Secondary: (a) *Gymnasio* for a duration of three years and (b) *Lykio* for a duration of three years. This is followed by a compulsory entrance examination to the tertiary level of education.
3. Tertiary: (a) *TEI (Teknologika Ekpedeftika Idrimata)* for a duration of three years; (b) *University,* leading to the first degree *(ptychio),* for four to six years' duration; and (c) *Professional Schools,* leading also to the first degree *(ptychio),* for four to six years' duration. They are the seven schools named above.
4. Post-Tertiary: (a) *Master's Degree,* two years' minimum duration and (b) *Doctorate,* two years' minimum duration.

Public education in Greece is fee-free and administered and funded by the Ministry of Education. Students are admitted to universities on the basis of their results in the Panhellenic Examinations, which are held every June. Students prepare themselves for many years for these exams, most by attending private schools *(frontistiria)* in addition to their public schooling. This exam is given at the same time all over the country at specified examination centers. It is the same exam for all students. The resultant grade places the student according to a hierarchy of schools matched against the student's preferences. For example, a student would have to score very well to enter the Philosophy School, which is among the highest within this hierarchy. With a low score, even if a preference were made for the school of philosophy, the student could only enter one of the schools requiring a lower grade.

Once admitted to a university, a student follows a prescribed curriculum of study. Attendance at classes during the academic year is not mandatory (nor expected). Grades in courses are based on a scale from 1-10, with 5 and above passing. Failure in a course is not detrimental to a student's standing. However, no credit is given and the course exam must be taken again until it is passed. A recent innovation has been to allow "continuous assessment" in place of the final exam that more or less establishes the entire grade for the class. This continuous assessment usually includes the writing of research papers and the taking of short examinations throughout the term. This option must be offered by the professor in order for the student to choose it. Since the grade is based in most cases only on a final exam, many students feel no need to attend classes and simply prepare for the final examination, taking it until it is passed. Exams are scheduled four times a year. This means that students need not necessarily finish the university degree within the four-year period, and there is no financial penalty for taking a longer time.[2]

In the normal course of events, instructors usually assign a reading list beyond the required texts (texts are provided free by the state). Books from this list are placed on reserve in the respective sectional or departmental library. With the educational atmosphere as described above, students are rarely encouraged to proceed beyond the use of these basic works. Further investigation is in fact hindered by the disorganized state of the libraries themselves. Thus, a pattern is established: the instructors don't encourage research because of the lack of library support; in turn, the lack of library support does not allow the instructors to assign work not dealt with in the required texts.

THE EVOLUTION OF ACADEMIC LIBRARIES

During the formative period in Greek higher education, the departmental structure was organized around the "professor." Each department was composed of several subdivisions called "sections." Each section usually had only one "professor," with the other faculty in lower ranks. A professor's power was manifested in many ways. One was in the acquisition of library materials, which were housed in the professor's office solely for his/her convenience. As a result, many small collections within departments, each called a "library," were formed. While the books belonged officially to the university, they were available, in essence, only to a few. This situation is now clearly illegal by Greek law, but the transition and subsequent transfer of these materials has been slow.[3] Although this situation is typical of the older institutions (Athens and Thessaloniki), the libraries within the newer schools–where professors wield less authority–have not developed this way. Central library systems were not traditional for Greek universities and are only encountered in a few of the newer institutions today.

Characteristic of the three newest universities (the Universities of the Aigaio, Ionio, and Thessalia) is the geographical separation of central administration offices, including the library, from each of the university campuses. All offices are located in Athens and will remain there until the university has elected a rector. The rector, a member of the faculty, must be elected by a vote of the faculty and students. It is very difficult for fledgling universities to properly support the research needs of the faculty and students when their libraries are located at a place physically distant. In addition to the library's physical separation from the campuses, the various schools of the universities are also dispersed. For example, the University of the Aegean has schools on four islands: in Lesvos, Hios, Samos, and Rodos.

EXAMINATION OF INDIVIDUAL LIBRARY SYSTEMS

Kapodistrian University of Athens

The University of Athens, founded in 1837, consists of nine schools, 24 departments, and approximately 45,000 students. Located in the heart of Athens, its buildings are scattered around the city. There is a new campus under construction outside the city where current plans call for eventual consolidation of all schools. The major collection of the university is housed together with the collections of the National Library. The National Library of Greece was founded in 1832 by Ioannis Kapodistrias, the first governor of the Greek state. The Library collects materials by means of a legal deposit law, requiring two copies of every publication (one copy for the National Library and another for the University). Since University deposit texts are not separated in any way from the National Library's texts, all fall under the realm of the National Library. In reality, this library does not function as a "central" library for the University. It does not exert, nor attempt to exert, any control over the decentralized library structure that services the various schools and departments. This structure consists of 50 libraries, both departmental and sectional. To exemplify the varied nature of these specialized libraries, a library of each type will now be examined.

Within the School of Philosophy, in the Department of Philology, is a section of Classical Philology. Its library of 70,000 monographic and serial volumes are classified using an in-house system, based on subject and accession number. Open daily from 8:30 a.m. to 2:30 p.m., this open-stack collection circulates materials to faculty, but not students.[4] The library's lone staff member is a graduate of the Athens TEI School of Librarianship.[5]

The collection of the French departmental library consists of 12,000 volumes that are not classified, but arranged in broad subject areas. The librarian intends to begin Dewey Decimal Classification (DDC), but confessed that he did not know how to assign subject headings and will consult with faculty for assistance. This open-stack library circulates material for 15 days to students and for an unlimited time to faculty. A staff of one, also a graduate of the TEI School of Librarianship, serves a student body of 1000 and a faculty of 20. The library is open from 8:30 a.m. to 2:30 p.m., Monday through Friday.[6]

In addition to the departmental libraries, there is the library of the "Student Center."[7] It functions as an adjunct library to the University. Its 30,000-volume collection consists primarily of texts and supplementary material from all departments. This closed-stack library with a non-circulating collection serves only students, not faculty. It is open from 8 a.m. to 9 p.m., Monday through Friday. A committee of students and faculty representing all schools will be formed for future collection development decisions.[8] The Student Center receives funding from the University as a separate department. Other parts of the student center include the medical clinic and student food services (all services, including food, are free to students).

Aristotelian University of Thessaloniki

The University of Thessaloniki, founded in 1925, consists of 12 schools and 36 departments. It is the largest university in Greece, with approximately 55,000 students. Buildings are centrally located in a campus setting. The library system consists of a Central Library, housed in its own building in the center of the campus, and approximately 245 separate libraries. These libraries vary in size of collection from 50 to 30,000 volumes. Some are departmental libraries, such as the English Department Library; others are university-owned collections housed in professors' offices or libraries of sections of departments. The Physics Department has several of these section collections, such as the Applied Physics collection, the Solid Physics collection, etc.

Within the School of Theology are two departments that contain many sections. Most of these sections maintain their own library collections. Father Nik Koursouloudis, a faculty member, describes the Applied Theology sectional library as typical: "There is no library staff; faculty of the School assist in daily operations . . . the real problem of libraries in Greece is that they are in desperate need of specialized and qualified librarians. Librarians are available, but these are not hired, since there are no positions available by the state. Therefore, professors and lecturers are obliged to undertake library and administrative duties."[9]

The Central Library is attempting to exert some control over these smaller libraries. This control is not budgetary, since each library receives funding from parent departments, but rather extends to the classification of materials. A computerized union catalog has been developed utilizing dBase II for periodical holdings. It is hoped that this will serve as a model for a union catalog for books at a later time.

Departments of the Central Library include Administration, Classification, Circulation, Bindery, and Interlibrary loans administered through the International Federation of Library Associations and Institutions (IFLA). The Library is governed by an eight-member committee that consists of five members of the faculty union, one member from civil service ranks, one student, and the Director of the Central Library, who functions as a chair. A collection of approximately 500,000 volumes and 3,500 periodical titles is housed in closed stacks. Materials circulate 15 days for students and a month for faculty and staff. The Library is open from 7:30 a.m. to 3:00 p.m., Monday through Friday. Study areas (but not library materials) are available to students from 3:30 p.m. to 8:30 p.m. Sixteen staff members make up the personnel. At this writing, none has a graduate degree in library science. There are only some with TEI diplomas in librarianship. The Director of the Library has a degree in law, and others hold university degrees in varying disciplines from (economics to philosophy). Dimitris Dimitriou, the Library Director, summarized this lack of professional expertise with the remark that "personnel is our biggest problem."[10]

University of Patra

The University of Patra, founded in 1964, consists of six schools and 16 departments in a campus setting outside the city. The Central Library was established in 1967. It maintains a circulating open-stack collection of 10,000 volumes (which are organized according to Universal Decimal Classification [UDC]) and it subscribes to 1,100 periodical titles. It serves a student body of 8,000, and is open from 7:30 a.m. to 2:30 p.m., Monday through Friday. Of a staff of five, only the Director has a university degree (in economics).

Under the provisions of Greek law, the Mathematics Department created its own library in 1985 by gathering together small collections once housed in professors' offices.[11] They have been actively acquiring specialized material in the field, avoiding duplication with the Central Library. Eventually, it is intended to withdraw all relevant books and periodicals from the Central Library and place them in the Mathematics Department. The Director of the Central Library fears that other departments will follow suit and thus relegate the role of the Central Library to a merely administrative one.[12]

University of Ioannina

The University of Ioannina, founded in 1964, consists of five schools and nine departments. At this time, the campus is in two locations. The one in the city houses the School of Philosophy, the

Central Library offices, and the administration of the university. The rest of the schools are located on a new campus outside the city. Eventually, all schools will move to this new campus, and there is provision for a central library building. The Central Library has no collection and functions only administratively. Departmental acquisitions are processed through this office by assigning author card and accession number to incoming books for the purposes of recordkeeping. The books are then dispersed to the various departments, which will catalog them in whatever system they have been using. Classification systems include the Universal Decimal Classification (UDC) and various in-house-produced systems.

The Mathematics Department maintains a 13,000-volume openstack collection. Materials circulate six months for faculty and 20 days for students. Students from other departments cannot borrow materials without special permission. Two staff members (one a graduate of the TEI School of Librarianship) service this collection from 7:30 a.m. to 2:30 p.m., Monday through Friday.[13] They are experimenting with a personal computer to handle word processing and to track acquisitions; they hope to eventually link up with the National Documentation Center in Athens.[14]

In the School of Philosophy, there are three departments. One of the departments, Philology, consists of three sections: Classical Philology, Medieval and Modern Philology, and Linguistics. Each has its own library collection. The library of the Classical Philology section will serve as an example. A closed-stack collection of 20,000 volumes circulates materials to students for three days. Faculty can borrow an unlimited number of books for as long as needed. This library is open from 8:30 a.m. to 1:30 p.m. and from 5 p.m. to 8 p.m., Monday through Friday. However, all faculty have keys, and thus have access to the collection at any time. The two library employees received their training on the job. Although there are plans to move to the new campus, there has been no provision for consolidation of all the sectional libraries of the School of Philosophy.[15]

Dimokritian University of Thraki

The University of Thraki, founded in 1973, consists of three separate campuses, with seven independent departments. The Law and Physical Education Schools are located in Komotini Campus.

The Polytechnic School, which consists of the Departments of Civil Engineering and Electronics, is located in Xanthi. These two campuses have well-maintained central libraries serving their departments. They both have open stacks and circulate collections of 65,000 at Komotini and 32,000 at Xanthi. While the library in Komotini has extensive hours for a Greek library (7 a.m. to 8 p.m., Monday through Friday), the Xanthi library is open only from 7 a.m. to 2:30 p.m. Both libraries are governed by seven-member committees, composed of professors, librarians, and students.

The independent departments of Elementary School Education, Pre-School Education, and Medicine are located in Alexandroupolis. The education departments are still in the planning stages. In their place is a two-year College of Elementary Education, which will be converted to the four-year university-level program. There is a library supporting this program, and it will eventually serve as the basis for the new institution's library. Moreover, until buildings and hospital facilities are completed in Alexandroupolis, the students of the Medical Department take classes at the University of Thessaloniki Campus.

At the University of Xanthi, computer technology is taught and professors have been experimenting with this technology for library applications. During the period of 1977-1979, a systems analyst developed software for producing catalog cards by using a Univac mainframe.[16] A circulation component will be a part of this automated system in the near future. Plans are to connect the system with the National Documentation Center in Athens.

University of Kriti

The University of Kriti, founded in 1973, consists of four schools and 18 departments. It is situated on two campuses in two cities: Rethimno and Iraklio, which are 78 km apart. The Philosophy School (consisting of three departments) is located in Rethimno, while the Schools of Pure and Applied Sciences and Health Sciences are located in Iraklio. The administrative offices of the university are located on the Rethimno campus. Both campuses have only central libraries, and these are administered by librarians with graduate degrees in Library Science. The Library of Congress Classification (LCC) scheme is used in both libraries. Bibliographic instruction and extended hours of operation (Iraklio, 7:30 a.m. to 8 p.m., Monday through Friday, and 9 a.m. to 1 p.m. on Saturday and Sunday; Rethimno, 7 a.m. to 8 p.m., Monday through Friday) are unique characteristics not shared by any other academic library in Greece. The two libraries also enjoy the benefits of computer technology. They are operating an integrated library system that was written and tested at the Iraklio facilities with the use of a minicomputer from the University's Computer Center.[17]

An intelligent grasp of the mission and the objectives of an academic library places these two libraries at the forefront of Greek academic libraries. They should stand as models for the rest of the country.

University of the Aigaio

The University of the Aigaio, founded in 1984, consists of six departments. Presently, only one of the departments functions on the island of Hios. Other departments will be located on the islands of Lesvos, Samos, and Rodos. Administrative offices, as well as the library offices, are located in Athens. Acquisitions and cataloging are processed in Athens, and materials are shipped to the island. The librarian in Athens has a graduate degree in Library Science and plans to initiate a computerized system for technical processing.[18]

University of Ionio

The University of Ionio, located on the island of Kerkira (Corfu) and founded in 1984, consists of four departments, of which only one currently functions. Administrative offices are located in Athens. The staff in Athens acquires and stamps books with an accession number for the department and ships the books to the island, where they will eventually be cataloged.

One of the planned departments would offer a program in archives management and librarianship. While original plans called for the opening of this department in the fall of 1987, several factors prevented this from happening. The paucity of qualified native teachers, combined with a recent Greek ruling that university professors and lecturers must be Greek citizens, restricts the possibilities for hiring faculty. Discussions with a member of the founding committee of this university revealed that they are very concerned about the problem of insufficient qualified personnel but, as yet, have no solutions to it.[19]

University of Thessalia

The University of Thessalia, founded in 1984, consists of two schools and eight departments. This University was established by parliamentary decree. Presently, none of its departments functions; no faculty has been hired, nor any students admitted. The administration is located in Athens.

LEGAL ASPECTS

One of the pertinent factors hindering the development of university libraries has been the lack of legislation specifically addressing library issues. As with any governmental institution in Greece, academic libraries cannot function without a legal framework, both establishing them and giving them their basis for operation. The New Frame Law of 1982, which pertains to "the structure and function of higher education institutions," devoted only a six-line paragraph on the subject of academic libraries: "By decision of the Senate following proposals of the Deans, department libraries can be established. The staff of the libraries belongs to the Special Administrative-Technical Staff of the Department or the Administrative Staff of the Higher Educational Institution. The decision on the appointment of this staff is made by the General Assembly of the Department or the Senate respectively."[20] This law places emphasis on the staffing of libraries, ignoring the operational functions of these institutions.

Two more extensive, but still inadequate, paragraphs were added to this law in 1983.[21] These new paragraphs stipulate that a central library may be established for each university, while at the same time allowing for departmental libraries. These departmental libraries will be created from a consolidation of the "collections" that have evolved from the former sections of that department. The 1983 law also stipulates that a presidential decree be written outlining specifics concerning the responsibilities of the central and departmental libraries. The complexity of the Greek legal system requires that the universities respond to the Ministry by either (1) accepting the law, (2) presenting suggestions for revisions, or (3) refusing to implement the law. So far, very little action has been taken by any university. It is the authors' impression that university administrations agree with the law, but cannot implement it because it contradicts other governmental policies. For example, the law provides for professional librarians to be hired. This has not happened for several reasons: in addition to the paucity of professional librarians, it is the government's policy not to hire permanent employees as an austerity measure.

Recognizing this absence of concern on the part of the Ministry and the inadequacy of the law addressing library issues, a committee was formed in June 1987. Ioannin Deliyannis, a former Rector of the University of Thessaloniki, was appointed to chair this seven-member committee of concerned librarians and university professors. Their charge was to present to the Ministry (by the end of October 1987) proposals concerning the function, administration, and staffing of academic libraries. A draft of these proposals clearly delineates the functions of both the central and departmental libraries. Authority for administration, acquisition, classification, preservation, and interlibrary loan (ILL) would reside with the central library. Departmental libraries would be responsible for the selection of materials, the housing of those materials, organization of the card catalogs, circulation, and bibliographic instruction.[22]

The final document of this committee, after review by the Greek Librarians' Association, will be presented to the Ministry, which will then bring it before the Parliament to become law. Professor Deliyannis is convinced that these proposals have a high likelihood of becoming law this time.

PROBLEM AREAS

The decentralized system that exists in most universities has forced the small departmental and sectional libraries to become autonomous and independent from one another. This isolation is dysfunctional and requires unnecessary duplication of many facets of the library process. The cases below exemplify some of the more problematic areas.

The exclusive nature of these individual libraries can be seen in their circulation policies. When they do circulate materials, they will circulate them only to the students of that department or section. The interdepartmental nature of many of the majors on any college campus shows how detrimental such a philosophy is to research activity. It is because of such a philosophy that duplication of resources has been necessary. For example, within the School of Law at the University of Athens are six separate sections, each with its own library. In addition to collecting in an area of specialization, each collects the same basic works and thus an unnecessary duplication of material occurs (and scarce money is wasted). Many people are cognizant of this particular problem, from directors of schools to the individual librarians and the students themselves. There is much talk about a consolidation of collections into departmental libraries, as allowed in the 1983 law. However, this is a very slow process, and it will likely continue for some time.

Duplication also extends to personnel. These small sectional libraries need at least one staff member; some have more. If these libraries were combined into one departmental library, fewer staff and extended hours of operation could be allowed. With such a vacuum of qualified professional librarians in Greece, larger and more consolidated libraries could take fuller advantage of available personnel.

There is much talk that computers will improve library operations and services. In addition to scarce funding, secrecy and suspicion among the librarians hinder the development of automated systems. Plans, programs, and software are developed independently in each library. Xanthi and Kriti are developing computer systems, and they both mention their wish to connect with the Athens Documentation Center, but not with each other. Without any cooperation and mutual plans, such an interface will be a difficult and slow process.

Cooperation, which is such an integral part of library service, is almost completely nonexistent. As a result, there is a continuance of the politically separate situation that exists in a decentralized university environment. Although a centralized system is traditionally American–and thus might not be applicable to Greece in quite the same way–perhaps a move toward a centralization of services within discrete units would be appropriate. For example, the five libraries in the School of Theology of Thessaloniki could combine into one library. This would eliminate personnel costs and duplicated reference and periodical sources. Of course, the primary reasons to implement such a change would be to increase patron satisfaction; to allow all materials to be classified in a similar manner and with properly trained personnel; and to create an atmosphere where learning and scholarly interaction may take place.

One of the comments made again and again by the people interviewed concerns lack of properly educated and trained personnel. Without a basic knowledge of library fundamentals, it is difficult to develop policies. It is for this reason that little or no reference service exists, few institutions have collection development policies, and there is a lack of understanding of the difficulty that short library hours create for students in borrowing materials.

Most officials in Greece are aware of these problems and are working toward a solution to them. The library committee chaired by Professor Deliyannis, if successful in its legal reform, will help considerably in alleviating some of the more salient political problems affecting academic libraries. The proposed School of Archives and Librarianship to be established on the island of Kerkira (within the University of Ionio) will provide the country with a pool of qualified librarians. With improved library service both to faculty and students, research in technology advances that Greece needs desperately will become more tangible.

AFTERWORD

The observations included in this article are based on research conducted in 1985-86. An interview team consisting of Nancy Birk, Dimitris Karageorgiou, and Scott L. Shafer[23] visited ninety-three academic, public, and special libraries in Greece.

Since that study was conducted, seven students from Aristotle University of Thessaloniki have been graduated from the Kent State

University School of Library Science and three librarians from Aristotle University Libraries have done "internships" at the Kent State Libraries. Countless hours have been spent in conversations and meetings with these Greek librarians about the current state of librarianship and future possibilities. Most of the problems addressed in this article are still problems, however. Some changes have occurred that make the educational system even more fraught with challenges. Continued, maybe even intensified, political unrest culminating in the inability of Greece to form a government in 1989-90 underscores all the difficulties the educational community is now suffering. It was not until after three disruptive national elections that a stable government was formed in April 1990. Intermittent strikes by secondary school teachers in 1990 and 1991 have caused delays in the Panhellenic examinations. The examination system itself has been called into question, and attempts to change this method of university entrance are now being considered.

Clearly, political and economic changes will continue to plague Greek academic libraries. Perhaps with the changes in the European Economic Community (EEC), in 1992 some stability might soon be possible.

REFERENCE NOTES

1. *International Library Review* 16 (July 1984): 235-246.
2. This causes a problem in compiling statistics, since no one really knows how many students are "enrolled" at any one time; as a result, rough estimates must be given.
3. Law 1404/83, Article 49, Paragraph 5a, p. 12.
4. Interview, Athens, June 5, 1986.
5. TEI, a technical training school (not a university), offers a diploma in librarianship. The Thessaloniki school, founded in 1981, has graduated approximately 40 students. The Athens school, founded in 1977, has graduated approximately 600.
6. Interview with Yorgos Rungeris, Athens, June 6, 1986.
7. "Fititiki Leschi Panepistimiou Athinon."
8. Interview with Evangelia Sifaki-Bakopanou, Athens, May 30, 1986.
9. Interview with Nik Koursouloudis, Thessaloniki, April 22, 1986.
10. Interview, Thessaloniki, April 16, 1986.
11. Law 1404/83, Article 49, Paragraph 5a, p. 12. This law will be explained more fully in the section on legal aspects.
12. Interview with Andreas Belekokias, Patra, June 9, 1986.

13. Interview with Yorgos Zahos, Ioannina, June 25, 1986.

14. The National Documentation Center was founded in 1977 as a joint program of UNESCO and the Greek government. Their project objectives include providing the necessary infrastructure for information services for all levels of the government. One of the first projects of this center has been to design an on-line union catalog of scientific and technical periodicals in Greek research libraries. It must be noted that no academic libraries are yet included.

15. Interview with Rapit Irini, Ioannina, June 25, 1986.

16. Pericles Papadoperakis, "The Automation Project at Library B of Thrace University," *Program* 16 (April 1981): 57-66.

17. Interview with Michael Tzekakis, Rethimno, June 3, 1986.

18. Interview with Aliki Tsukala, Athens, April 30, 1986.

19. Interview with K. Kandris, Athens, June 21, 1986.

20. Law 1268/82. Article 7, Paragraph 7, p. 28.

21. Law 1404/83, Article 49, Paragraph 5a, p. 12.

22. Telephone interview with Ioannis Deliyannis, Thessaloniki, September 8, 1987.

23. Mr. Shafer is Head of Public Services at the Lima, Ohio, Public Library.

Library Education in Greece

Mersini Moreleli-Cacouris

BACKGROUND

Modern Greek library history has its origins in the late eighteenth century. The first libraries were established in the period known as the Greek Enlightenment (i.e., while Greece was still under the Turkish yoke). These first libraries were school libraries. With the emergence of the modern Greek state, however, they fell into inactivity and oblivion, as if they had completed their cycle of awakening the Greek people against their oppressors.

A landmark in the history of libraries of the modern Greek state is the establishment, in 1832, of the National Library of Greece on the island of Aegina, off Piraeus. This occurred almost simultaneously with the emergence of the independent Greek state, and even before Athens itself had become the capital of the country.[1] The first librarian of this library, George Gennadius, an eminent scholar, was appointed in 1832.[2] Obviously, he had no specialized library training. This practice of appointing scholars or bibliophiles to head the National Library, though valid for almost all libraries in the world at that time and later, has continued to the present date and is probably the chief reason for the inertia that characterizes its activities.

In 1838, the first academic library, that of the University of Athens, was established. In 1842, its collection was merged with that of the National Library. Georgios Kozakes Typaldos, a scholar and bibliophile, was appointed as director, and he administered both libraries. Sixty years later, in 1903, the National Library moved to a new building in the center of Athens.[3]

As the university of Athens expanded its schools and programs, seminar collections were developed, administered by the chairs or departments, and serviced by either administrative staff or assistants to the chairs. The result of this process was that no central library developed, there was no university librarian, and more important, there was no need, in the minds of the central university administration and professors, for professional librarians and, therefore, professional training.

If one bears in mind that until 1925 this was the only university in the country and that the National Library never felt the need for professional training, one understands why professional library training did not emerge until much later. This picture has undergone changes during the latter half of the twentieth century. But, even though courses in librarianship have been offered for almost 30 years, there is still some confusion both in the minds of the general public and the authorities as to what a librarian is, what he or she does, and what kind of training, if any, he or she needs. The notion that a holder of a university degree in any discipline can work not only as a librarian but also teach specialized courses in a library school still widely exists.[4] In addition, the notion is expressed that librarianship is a technical vocation, and the level and type of this vocation is similar to that, say, of a dental technician.[5]

PRE-1977 LIBRARY EDUCATION

At this point, it is of interest to consider what preceded the establishment of the first state library science department in 1977. The early part of the twentieth century might be considered a desert insofar as library training goes. In 1949, a law concerning the "foundation, reformation, and uniform organization of Greek libraries" stated for the first time, among other things, the need for library training.[6] An article of this law, under the title "Library science studies cycle," provided that the National Library was to undertake this task.[7] Details concerning the length of studies, the curriculum, and faculty requirements were to be specified in subsequent decrees. These decrees, however, never saw the light of day. As a consequence, in the absence of locally trained personnel, for years Greek libraries were staffed either with administrative staff with no library training or with graduates mainly of American and British library schools.

The 1950s were marked by a series of very brief, one-to-two day (occasionally longer) training courses for library employees in state and local government agencies. The early 1960s were noted for two substantive developments. The first was that the Greek state, through the Ministry of Education, sought advice from the United Nations Educational, Scientific, and Cultural Organization (UNESCO) on establishing formal library training programs at the university level. In 1960 and 1962, two UNESCO-appointed experts, Dr. Leon Carnovsky (Professor at the Graduate Library School of the University of Chicago) and Dr. Preben Kirkegaard (Rector of the Royal Danish School of Librarianship), after local visits and assessments, recommended the establishment of Library Science Departments at the schools of Philosophy of the University of Athens and the University of Thessaloniki, respectively.[8] These recommendations never materialized, and probably were never seriously taken into consideration by the then-relevant government agencies.

The second significant development of the 1960s was the establishment, in September 1961, of the first library vocational school by the Athens YWCA as part of its vocational training programs.[9] This was a one-year program that continued through June 1977, the year when the first state library science department was established. The majority of those who attended this school were either working in libraries or were holders of a university degree who wished to pursue a new career. The faculty were practicing librarians, with professional qualifications from abroad, and active in the profession. In total, 288 librarians were trained in the YWCA library school.[10] It can now be assessed that their impact on library organization and development in the Athens area has been quite significant. A possible criticism one might have of the YWCA library school is that because of the short length of its program–October through June–the scope of its curriculum was rather small. Also, because almost all of its students came from the Athens area, its impact and influence on the national library scene was limited.[11]

POST-1977 LIBRARY EDUCATION

The year 1977 is the most significant landmark in the history of library training as a state responsibility. New institutions of tertiary education were established in 1977. At the time, these were called "Centers of Higher Technical Education" (in Greek, KATE). In 1977, they were renamed "Centers of Higher Technical and Professional Education" (in Greek, KATEE). As of 1983, they have been called "Technological Education Institutes" (in Greek, TEI). These changes in name reflect a substantial evolving of these institutions in terms of goals and objectives. One might safely say that the present TEI roughly correspond to the British Polytechnics.

Law No. 1404 in 1983, known as Law 1404/83, which made possible the transition and upgrading of the KATEE into the TEI, explicitly describes the function of these institutions to "offer theoretical and practical education, appropriate for the application of scientific, technological, artistic or other kind of knowledge and skills, and assist in the formation of responsible citizens who will be able to contribute, as application cadres . . . to the economic, social, and cultural development of the country. . . ."[12]

A distinction between the role of the TEI and that of universities was also made. Whereas education at the TEI would focus on the assimilation and application of already accumulated knowledge, universities would focus "on the development of science, on research, and on higher theoretical and global training."[13] The establishment of these new state institutions to provide substantive professional and technical training outside a university, mostly for the emerging new professions, made it possible for a Department of Library Science to be established within the first KATEE, that of Athens. The Department, offering a six-semester, three-academic-year program, was incorporated into what may be called the Business and Management School of that institution. Following the same model, a Department of Library Science was established in Thessaloniki in 1981.

THE STUDENTS

Education in Greece is provided at three levels: *Elementary* (six years); *Secondary* (three years at the *gymnasio* and three years at the *lykeio*); and *tertiary*. The six years of elementary school and the three years of the *gymnasio* are compulsory; tertiary education takes place at the universities, TEI, military academies, and institutes of technology. State education at all levels is completely free, and includes tuition, textbooks, and, for the majority of students at the tertiary level, free meals.

The management of the system is centralized. The Ministry of National Education and Religion sets up the curricula, appoints and pays teachers, and is in general responsible for the administering of the country's education programs. The concept of the one textbook for every subject, the same in all primary and secondary schools, prevails throughout the country and at every educational level.[14]

Students are admitted to any tertiary educational institution on the basis of scores achieved in the so-called Panhellenic (or General) Examinations. There are four options in these Panhellenic Examinations, each leading to a group of disciplines offered by the universities and the TEI. The first option is the schools of engineering, physics, chemistry, etc.; the second, the biomedical sciences (medicine, dentistry, biology, nursing, etc.); the third, philosophy, literature, languages, theology, and law; and the fourth, economics and political and social sciences. This latter group, the fourth option, includes the library science departments.

Senior high school students decide which option they wish to take, and the university and the TEI departments they wish to enter. These might be as many as eighty-five in the first option, for example, and as diverse as philosophy and midwifery.[15] It is to be noted that the majority of the students list university departments as their first choice, since the social status and image of the TEI is lower than that of the university. Also, the notion still exists that a university degree offers more and better career opportunities and prestige.

At the end of their senior year, students take the state examination. On the basis of their performance and their comparative scores against other candidates, they are admitted to a university or a TEI department of their first, second, or even last choice. The data is processed electronically at the national level. It is obvious that the personality, the background, or the special interests of each student are ignored.

Students are examined in four subjects, which are different for each option. One of these is the basic subject, failure in which disqualifies the candidate. Library science department candidates take examinations in history, sociology, essay writing, and mathematics. Mathematics is the basic subject in their option. It is of interest to note that of the 250 students admitted to the Thessaloniki Library Science Department during the academic years 1987-88 and 1988-89, only 193 registered. Table 1 shows these registrants' order of preference for admission to the department.[16]

The faculty of the library science department of Thessaloniki, its graduates, and students believe and have recommended that students from all four options should have the opportunity to apply to the department, since a variety of interests and backgrounds is essential to the future development of Greek librarianship. The department has also suggested the replacement of mathematics as the basic subject with English. The lack of library science literature in Greek and the high percentage, in most cases over 70 percent, of material in English in academic and special libraries make the knowledge of English essential for Greek librarians. The final decision in this matter, however, has to be made by the relevant authority in the Greek Ministry of Education.

In 1990-1991, a total of 124,658 students took the state examinations. Of those, 23,205 were admitted to university and 18,974 to TEI departments, of which 125 and 120 enrolled in the Thessaloniki and the Athens library science departments, respectively.[17] In addi-

TABLE 1. Student Preference for Admission to the Library Science Department

Order of preference for Library Science Dept.	Number of students who expressed the preference	Percentage
1st	9	4.7
2nd	15	7.8
3rd	10	5.2
4th	12	6.2
5th	8	4.1
6th-10th	37	19.2
11th-15th	24	12.5
16th-20th	32	16.5
21st-25th	26	13.5
26th-30th	8	4.1
31st-35th	10	5.2
36th-38th	2	1.0

tion, about 10 percent of this number, holders of a university degree, may be admitted to the Library Science Department every year at the discretion of the department faculty.

THE CURRICULUM

The aims of the programs offered at the KATEE are broadly and vaguely stated as follows in the foundation law: "the schools aim at offering the necessary theoretical and practical knowledge, so that the graduates become employees of a higher level, thus contributing to the development of certain sections of the national economy. . . ."[18] There are no specific aims and objectives for each department that would lead to, and develop, more rational curricula to serve the real needs of each profession. Partly because of this, the curriculum of the newly founded library science department in the Athens KATEE in 1977 was not balanced, and there were no stated aims and objectives for each course. Neither were there course contents listed. At the same time, a clause in the law made it possible for KATEE graduates to be admitted to universities on the basis of special examinations administered by the universities themselves. This stunted the curriculum and justified the teaching of non-library courses in the form of electives in order to achieve this objective.

The social status of a university student and graduate, the once-present uncertainty of employment of a library department graduate, the low incentive and chance admission of students on the basis of scores achieved in the General Examinations, and optional attendance all acted as counter-incentives to substantive teaching. With the establishment of the TEI, the curriculum was changed. Suggestions made by the Greek Library Association and the faculty of the Athens department of library science were taken into consideration. New courses were introduced, and course contents were outlined.[19] The new four-year program included six semesters of course work, six calendar months of practicum, and the submission of a thesis.

There are, as in all the TEI departments, 32 weekly periods of course work for each semester, but, according to internal regulations, students can take as many as 45 periods of course work a week. This may be a world record for students at the tertiary education level. The majority of students opt for a 45-period-a-week load. They cannot, consequently, attend all classes or participate actively in the educational process. Current recommendations developed by the faculty of the Thessaloniki department, after consultation with head librarians and graduates in the field, require students to take a maximum of 20 periods a week and attend all classes.[20]

THE STAFF

University and TEI faculties are staffed according to *loi-cadre*, which also regulates their function. Positions are advertised nationally, and candidates are elected by a body appointed by either the departments–in cases when at least seven members have already been appointed–or by the parent institutions. According to the *loi-cadre* for the KATEE, a university first degree, in a discipline relevant to the position to be filled, three years of professional experience and two years of teaching experience were the minimum prerequisites for appointment to a position in any of the departments.[21] Again, according to that law, basic relevant degrees for appointment to the library science departments were those from university schools of philosophy, literature, history, theology, political science, and law, among others. Library experience was vaguely defined. So, initially, the Athens department of library science was staffed with graduates who had, as a rule, no real library experience whatsoever.

The overall picture of library training of that period was not very promising. There were students who had been almost accidentally admitted to a department and a profession that they hardly understood and who operated in an unwelcoming and uninspiring physical and intellectual environment. What's more, these classes were taught by an underqualified and uninterested faculty who could not contribute positively to the development of the new profession. The quality of training at the KATEE was heavily criticized by the Greek Library Association, librarians, graduates, and students.[22] This criticism, however, did not only apply to the library science department but also to most of the KATEE schools.

As a result of this pervasive assessment, the KATEE were remodeled, reorganized, and renamed TEI in 1983. Although the TEI

were new institutions, basically the same departments were included, and all the KATEE staff were reappointed to the TEI departments. At that time, the Greek Library Association expressed its
objections and reservations as to the establishment of a library
science department within the TEI It was believed that the orientation of the department would be distorted, since all major decisions
concerning staffing and other future developments would be taken
over by people outside the library profession.[23] The following were
suggested by the Association as the minimum requirements for a
library science program:

- Independent library schools.
- Qualified staff, elected by library professionals.
- Motivated and interested students.
- National survey of information needs for better overall plan-
  ning.[24]

None of these suggestions was accepted by the Ministry of Education. This can be easily understood when the overall structure and
philosophy of Greek public administration is taken into consideration.

However, at the TEI, despite the objections expressed, faculty
requirements for new appointments were upgraded and their qualifications were clearly stated, a great improvement over its predeces-
sor institution, the KATEE. There are now three levels of teaching
staff, each level having its own minimum requirements:

1. *Professors*, who must have: a doctoral degree relevant to the
   position to be filled; ten years of professional experience;
   publications; and four years of teaching experience at the tertiary educational level.
2. *Assistant professors*, who must have: a master's degree relevant to the position to be filled; seven years of professional
   experience; publications; and two years of teaching experience
   at the tertiary educational level.
3. *Laboratory teachers*, who must have: a TEI degree; a specialization degree; and eight years of professional experience. In
   addition, all candidates must know a foreign language.[25]

Unfortunately, the candidate's personality and teaching and communication abilities are not considered at all.

Although the new requirements seem to be in the right direction, there are cases, as with the Thessaloniki library science department, where candidates possessing the full qualifications for permanent appointment are not available in the field. As a result, the department has to lean heavily on temporary, part-time appointments on terms that are centrally regulated.

THE GRADUATES

There are to date (1990) 506 graduates of the Athens Library Science Department and 238 of the Thessaloniki department. Recently, the state–in explicitly sanctioning the "professional rights" of librarians–has made it mandatory to appoint holders of library degrees to professional positions.[26]

Despite the absence of any reliable national statistical data, it is known that of the graduates of the TEI of Thessaloniki who are employed, most are in public libraries in the Thessaloniki metropolitan area or in Northern Greece. In almost all cases, they are the first library professionals appointed to these libraries, and it is safe to say that they are making a significant contribution to their development.

From May to September 1990, a survey concerning academic libraries was conducted. Questionnaires were sent to 123 central, departmental, and chair libraries that could be traced (there is no reliable data on the number, especially of departmental and chair libraries). Sixty-five libraries, 52.8 percent, responded to the questionnaire. The number of TEI graduates employed in these libraries is shown in Table 2. This is only a quantitative figure. A qualitative assessment as to their contribution is difficult to make at this stage, because (1) in most cases these are recent appointments and (2) none of these appointments is at a decision-making level.

CONCLUSION

Looking back over the past fourteen years (1977-1990) of state library education in Greece and the changing library scene, one can

TABLE 2. Qualifications of 139 Library Staff Members in 65 Central or Departmental Academic Libraries

Qualifications	Number of staff	Percentage
Ph.D. (no library qualifications)	2	1.4
M.L.S.	4	2.9
T.E.I.L.S. degree plus B.A. in other disciplines	5	3.6
TEI graduates	28	20.1
B.A. in L.S.	1	0.7
B.A. in any discipline except Lib. Sc.	44	31.7
YWCA Library School diploma	3	2.1
High-school diploma	52	37.4
TOTAL	139	

safely say that the contribution of the graduates of library science departments in the development of public and academic libraries is positive. In addition, a number of its graduates contribute to library education as part-time members of the teaching staff in the two departments, Athens and Thessaloniki.

The two departments have progressed significantly since their inception, and they continue to do so. The fact that they are situated in the two largest cities of the country enables them to function in an environment where there are considerable advantages for such institutions, namely:

1. A sufficient number of libraries of all types: academic, public, and special, where students may (a) fulfill the six-month practicum requirement toward graduation, (b) work on their assignments and theses, and (c) eventually be employed.
2. Institutions of higher education, from whose faculty the departments can draw personnel to teach special courses for which there are no full-time employment opportunities according to the curriculum.
3. Large libraries, from whose qualified staff the departments can fill vacancies in teaching staff positions, as these occur.

However, the negative aspects of the curriculum, the methods of its improvement and modernization, and the haphazard state-controlled student admission process have to be greatly improved. The Ministry of Education must disengage itself from having the last word on curriculum improvement and development and pass this responsibility over to the departments. Furthermore, it must allow for curriculum diversification between the two departments on the basis of evaluations and decisions of their own faculties. In addition, the faculty teaching load must be reduced to allow time for study and research. The present teaching load of 14 to 16 hours a week for professors and assistant professors, respectively, acts as a deterrent to such activities.

At present, there is no satisfactory provision for holders of a university degree in other disciplines to pursue a satisfactory program in library science, although such a need exists widely. A graduate program for such candidates must be instituted and must be flexible, so as to attract promising recent university graduates or library staff members with non-library science degrees who wish to specialize. Such a program for this type of graduate, if it is of a year's duration, will improve service in libraries and enrich the library scene. At the same time, this graduate program will allow TEI library science graduates to further pursue their studies. The program for university and TEI graduates should be diversified. In other words, the former must only take library science courses, while the latter might also take courses in other disciplines along with their library science courses.

REFERENCE NOTES

1. Dim, Margari, *Vivliologia kai Vivliothiconomia* [*Bibliology and Library Science*] (Athinai: Genikon Symvoulion Vivliothimkon tis Ellados, 1939), p. 162.
2. Ibid., p. 163.
3. Ibid., pp. 163-165.
4. TEI of Thessaloniki, School of Management and Economics, Internal Records.
5. Kostas Georgousopoulos, *"Pou kai Pos to Kyros"* ["Where and How the Status"] *Nea* (Athens), (June 19, 1987):27.
6. Compulsory Law 1362/49, *Peri Idryseos, Anasygrotiseos kai Eniaias Organoseos ton ana to Kratos Vivliothikon* [On the Foundation, Reformation and Uniform Organization of Libraries in the Country], *Efimeris tis Kyverniseos tou Vasileiou tis Ellados* A 337, article 19, (1949) pp. 975-980.
7. Ibid., p. 979.

8. George Cacouris, "Library education in Greece," *Encyclopedia of Library and Information Science* (NY: Marcel Dekker, 1973), vol. 10, p. 191.

9. Ibid., pp. 192-193.

10. El. Chrysina, *"O Vivliothicarios: Ena Meson gia ten Pnevmatiki Anaptyxe"* ["The Librarian: a Means toward Intellectual Development"]. *Neoi Orizontes* (Athens) IO:174 174 (September-October, 1978): 11.

11. Of its 288 graduates, only two were from Thessaloniki, and a few more were from towns outside of Athens.

12. *Technologika Ekpaideftika Idrymata: Enas Chronos Meta* [*Technological Education Institutes: a Year Later*] (Athina: E.Y.TEI, 1984), p. 29.

13. Ibid., p. 548.

14. This could offer an explanation for the lack of school libraries and for the bad organization of most academic libraries in Greece.

15. Presidential Decree 57/89, *Eisagogi Spoudaston sto Pronto Etos Spoudon ton Scholon kai Tmimaton . . . me to Systima ton Genikon Exetaseon . . .* [Student Admission to the First Year of Studies of the Schools and Departments . . . via the General Examinations . . .], *Efimeris tis Kyverniseos tis Ellinikis Dimokratias*, A 24, (1989) pp. 157-167.

16. Thessaloniki Library Science Dept., Student records.

17. *"Apotelesmata Exetaseon ton Anotaton kai Anoteron Ekpaideftikon Idrymaton"* ["Results of the Examinations to Higher Education Institutions"], *Makedonia* (Thessaloniki) (September 13, 1990): 1.

18. Law 576/77, *Peri Organoseos kai Dioikiseos tis Mesis kai Anoteras Technikis kai Epangelmatikis Ekpaidefseos* [On the Organization and Administration of Higher Technical and Professional Education], *Efimeris tis Kyverniseos tis Ellinikis Dimokratias*, A 192, article 25, (1977) p. 799.

19. See appendix for TEI Library Science Dept. course listing.

20. Thessaloniki Library Science Dept., Minutes of General Assembly Meeting, no. 31, December 4, 1989.

21. Law 575/77, *Peri Organoseos kai Dioikiseos tis Mesis kai Anoteras Technikis kai Epangelmatikis Ekpaidefseos*, article 33, p. 800.

22. *"Syzitisi peri Ellinikon Vivliothikon"* ["Round Table on Greek Libraries"] *Grammata kai technes* (Athens), nos. 28-29 (April-May 1984): 16-17; and Kostas Vasileiou, *"Ekpaidefsi ton Vivliothikarion"* ["Library Education"], *Vivliothikes kai Pliroforisi* (Athens) 1 (July 1984): 19.

23. Greek Library Association Report to the Ministry of Education Concerning the TEI. *Loi-cadre*, July 30, 1983.

24. Ibid.

25. *Technologika Ekpsideftika Idrymata*, pp. 56-58.

26. Presidential Degree 385/89, *Kathorismos Epangelmatikon Dikaiomaton Ptychiouchon tou Tmimatos Vivliothikonomias tis Scholis Dioikisis kai Oikonomias ton Technologikon Ekpaideftikon Idrymaton* [Professional Rights Definition of Graduates of the Library Science Department of the School of Management and Economics of the Technological Education Institutes], *Efimeris tis Kyverniseos tis Ellinikis Dimokratias*, A 169, (1989) p. 4099.

APPENDIX

TECHNOLOGICAL EDUCATION INSTITUTE (TEI)
OF THESSALONIKI

FACULTY OF ADMINISTRATION AND ECONOMICS
Department of Librarianship

1st Semester	Hours Theory	Lab
1 Foundations of librarianship	3	-
2 History of libraries	4	-
3 Descriptive Cataloging I	3	1
4 Educational Sociology	4	-
5 Greek Literature I	3	-
6 Reference sources and reference work	2	-
7 Greek Typing	-	2
8 Classification I	3	1
9 Reader's psychology	3	-

2nd Semester	Hours Theory	Lab
1 Types of libraries	3	-
2 Descriptive Cataloging II	1	3
3 Classification II	1	3
4 Greek general reference sources	2	2
5 Greek Literature II	3	-
6 Printing, publishing, reprography	4	-
7 English Typing	-	2
8 English I	3	1
9 French I–German I	3	1

3rd Semester	Hours Theory	Lab
1 Descriptive Cataloging III	2	2
2 Foreign general reference sources	2	2
3 World Literature I	3	-
4 Principles of Management	3	-
5 History of Writing	2	-
6 Classification III	1	3
7 English II	2	-
8 French II-German II	3	1
9 Collection Development and Technical Services of Libraries	4	-

4th Semester	Hours Theory	Lab
1 Library Administration	4	-
2 World Literature II	3	-
3 History of Greek Printing	3	-
4 Subject Indexing I	1	3
5 Descriptive Cataloging IV	2	2
6 Reference sources in the Social Sciences	3	3
7 Children's Literature	3	-
8 English III	3	1
9 French III-German III	3	1

5th Semester	Hours Theory	Lab
1 Archive Studies I	3	-
2 Documentation	2	3
3 Reference sources in the Humanities I	2	2
4 Introduction to Computers	2	-
5 Audio-visual Material	1	1
6 Subject Indexing II	1	3
7 Reference sources in the Pure and Physical Sciences	2	2
8 French-German for librarians	3	1
9 English for librarians	3	1

6th Semester	Hours Theory	Lab
1 Archive Studies II	3	-
2 Reference sources in the Humanities I	1	3
3 Documentation Centres	2	2
4 Library Automation	2	2
5 Communication-Public Relations	4	-
6 Reference sources in the Applied Sciences	1	1
7 Public libraries	4	-
8 School libraries	4	-
9 Academic libraries or special libraries	4	-
10 Seminar	3	-

Library Automation in Greece:
A Visitor's Perspective

Michael Kreyche

INTRODUCTION

Very little has been written, in English at least, about library automation in Greece. Papadoperakis has described in some detail a batch system developed at the University of Thrace during 1977-1979 to print catalog cards, a subject index, a short title list, and a serial holdings list.[1] Perhaps the most interesting aspect of this system is that records were stored in a Machine Readable Cataloging (MARC) format. The majority of the records, in fact, were loaded from tapes purchased from the British Library, and the remainder were punched from catalogers' worksheets coded with MARC content designation. Brief mention of this system has also been made by Krikelas[2] and Birk and Karageorgiou.[3] In their article, the latter authors profile libraries at the University of Thrace and eight other Greek universities, and mention automation in connection with four of these other eight: the Universities of Thessaloniki, Ioannina, Crete, and the Aegean. More recently, various aspects of the development of an on-line information retrieval service at the National Hellenic Research Foundation have been described.[4,5]

Based on the experience of spending the fall semester of 1989 at Aristotle University of Thessaloniki (AUT) as a participant in the exchange program with Kent State University, further detail will be presented here on automation activity at Thessaloniki and Crete, as well as observations on the prospects for library automation in Greece in general. The reader should also refer to the article by Bokos, published elsewhere in this volume, describing the initiative to automate the National Library of Greece, which is certain to have a profound influence on the course of library automation everywhere in Greece.

ARISTOTLE UNIVERSITY OF THESSALONIKI

Computerization of the Central Library of AUT began in late 1985 with the hiring of a full-time computer specialist, Paschalis Raptis. Two systems, one for serials control and the other for cataloging monographs, were developed using a Database Management System (DBMS) running under CCP/M. Later, the databases were transferred to IBM PC-compatible hardware, and the software was rewritten using a dBase III-compatible compiler.

The serials system, now on a stand-alone PC, is used to track subscriptions and produce a printed list of serials holdings and other reports. The cataloging database currently resides on a file server with three stations networked to it, and it has grown to about 20,000 records. The cataloging records contain fields for author, title, imprint, call number, various control numbers, a code for the department that ordered the title, and two subject headings. Access is provided by author and title.

While the latter system has some of the elements of a rudimentary on-line catalog, it was not intended to replace the card catalogs; it is used primarily to answer queries about in-process materials and to publish accession lists. These are produced in book form and are distributed throughout the University. The system is also used to print lists of ISBNs for ordering catalog cards. An obvious potential use of the database would be to print cards directly, but development of this capability was delayed in anticipation of using Online Computer Library Center (OCLC) for card production.

The installation of an OCLC terminal, accomplished in September 1989, was suggested and initiated by Evelina Smith, a colleague from the Trumbull Campus of Kent State University, who participated in the exchange in 1987 and 1988. This was the first, and remains to date the only, OCLC installation in Greece. After three days of carefully planned and well-conducted training sessions by Tina van Zeller, Marketing and Support Librarian from OCLC Europe, the staff of the Central Library began using the system. The advantages of switching from the manual procedures were immediate and dramatic. Stacks of books that would have taken days to catalog manually were disposed of in minutes, and interlibrary loan requests that had been submitted several times without success over a period of months on the basis of guesswork were fulfilled in a matter of weeks.

The adoption of OCLC was not without its difficulties, however. The lack of sufficiently trained library staff makes it impossible at present for the Central Library to undertake the obligations of full membership in OCLC, particularly to contribute original cataloging. As a "special user," the Central Library pays a premium for OCLC's on-line cataloging service. Instead of paying a per-record charge, the Library pays a steep per-search charge (about US$1.00 in the fall of 1989). The North American bias of the On-line Union Catalog makes this method of charging even more of a burden than it might seem. Since a large proportion of the University's acquisitions are European imprints, the hit rate against the OCLC database is lower than it typically is for U.S. or Canadian libraries. The alternatives are to pay for an inordinate number of unsuccessful searches or to limit OCLC cataloging to titles that seem most likely to be found.

Other problems are related to telecommunications. It is difficult to take advantage of the support provided by OCLC Europe, since it is almost impossible to put a telephone call through during working hours. Even when possible, international telephone calls from Greece are extremely expensive. The data connection to the OCLC database, though generally reliable and fast, is sometimes unstable during peak hours, and any disconnect while editing a record means paying for yet another search to retrieve the record again after the connection is reestablished.

The accumulation of a few years' experience with automation at the Central Library of AUT naturally led to aspirations of developing more sophisticated systems and extending services to departmental libraries and other offices on campus. To meet short-term needs, work was begun on a microcomputer program that would provide a MARC-based catalog and circulation capabilities for small departmental collections. In the longer term, plans were made to develop a minicomputer-based system that would connect to a campus network being developed with funding from the European Economic Community.

These initiatives progressed slowly for a time, due to the lack of personnel and the press of maintaining the existing systems. They came to a temporary halt in the fall of 1989, when Paschalis Raptis went to Kent State University to study for a master's degree in Library Science. During 1990, a pilot project to automate the Physics Department library using software developed at the University of Crete was initiated, with a view to adopting the system in the Central Library for materials held everywhere on campus. Many of the records from Crete were mounted on the system to facilitate conversion, and this has also stimulated some interlibrary loan activity.

UNIVERSITY OF CRETE

At about the same time that the library automation work was begun at AUT, a more ambitious development project was undertaken at the University of Crete by Janet Tavernaraki, head of the library at the Iraklion campus, and Grigoris Tzanodaskalakis, an analyst with the University's computer center. The result of this effort was an on-line cataloging and circulation system, sometimes referred to as *Ptolemeos*, which runs on an IBM 4361 minicomputer under VM/CMS and uses the SQL/DS database management system and COBOL with embedded SQL commands.

The bibliographic database is based on a nearly full implementation of United States Machine Readable Cataloging (USMARC), and now contains about 35,000 records. Many of these were loaded from tapes purchased from a commercial vendor in the United States, while others, particularly the Greek titles, were entered manually. The character set of the IBM terminals used on the system contains upper- and lower-case letters of both the Greek and Latin[6] alphabets. The keyboards can be toggled between alphabets, and they include "dead" keys for diacritics, so Greek and a number of other languages can be entered easily and displayed correctly.

The system's user interface is menu-driven and includes Help screens. The catalog can be searched by author, title, author/title, and subject using OCLC-like search keys, as well as by various control numbers and by keyword. Public bibliographic displays are in a labelled format, and item-level holdings are shown complete with circulation status.

Further development envisioned for the system includes acquisitions, serials control, and authorities functions. While some work can be expected to continue on the existing system, most effort will go into a complete reimplementation on a different hardware and software platform, using 4th Generation Language (4GL) facilities. The intent is to produce a system that is flexible and portable enough so that it can be promoted for use elsewhere in Greece.

AUTOMATION OPTIONS
FOR GREEK LIBRARIES

At the present time, there are very few options available to libraries in Greece that want to automate. The obvious solution for many libraries in countries with a well-developed library automation market–buying a turnkey system–is not so simply applied in Greece. Without any Greek-developed library automation systems available, the librarian is forced to look to the international market, which entails problems of its own.

The first problem is that international vendors of library systems, with some justification, have not found it worth their while to market their products in Greece. In some instances, computer hardware vendors have suggested library applications as an inducement to buy their products, but it is largely up to the Greek librarian to learn what products are available and determine how suitable they are. The difficulties and expense of international travel, telephone calls, and postal delivery compound the usual challenges of such an undertaking. The first requirement for any system imported from another country is the need to handle the Greek alphabet. The implications of this requirement are pervasive, affecting hardware, telecommunications, data entry, display, storage, indexing, and searching. All this means that the library and the vendor will have to come to an agreement on specifications, the development and testing process, and bearing the additional cost.

Yet another problem associated with buying systems from outside Greece is posed by restrictions on transferring funds abroad.

Sending payments out of the country is a difficult process, even for routine transactions such as purchasing books. At AUT, this is a primary obstacle to providing an on-line search service and to taking fuller advantage of the OCLC Interlibrary Loan system by ordering materials from commercial vendors and other agencies that require payment. Finally, there is the whole question of product support once a system has been installed, as was mentioned earlier in the discussion of the OCLC installation at Thessaloniki.

This catalog of difficulties is not meant to discourage either Greek librarians from purchasing library systems from outside the country or vendors from marketing library systems in Greece. The first few endeavors of this sort should be watched closely, because if they succeed, it will be much easier for other libraries to purchase these same systems. Included in this category are the project at the National Library, as described by George D. Bokos, and plans at the University of the Aegean to abandon its batch programs in favor of a microcomputer-based system.[7] From the perspective of vendors in the United States and other countries where there is a rapidly saturating library automation market, the potential for installing systems in Greece seems a perfect example of the new markets that are frequently held up as vital to the future economies of these countries.

The alternative to buying a system is to develop one in-house, as was done in the cases of the Universities of Thrace, Thessaloniki, and Crete. Generally speaking, undertaking the development of a system should be considered a last resort, something to do when there is no application otherwise available to do the job. Given the problems of finding and procuring a library automation system that meets the needs of Greek libraries, it is not surprising that this last resort might seem the only viable recourse.

The most important factor in the success of developing a system is a full appreciation of the complexity of the task. For the administrator, this means understanding that a substantial amount of staff resources must be dedicated to the project, and that it may take a considerable length of time to see useful results. This may be hard to accept without prior experience with automation. For the librarian, it means the need to thoroughly understand the principles of library operations and the details of the processes being automated;

to appreciate the importance of standards; and to be able to envision alternate approaches to a problem. All these requirements are hard to put together without professional training, broad experience, and some familiarity with computer systems. Programmers and analysts must develop an appreciation of the special difficulties of library automation. The textual nature of bibliographic data, with its variable-length fields, the arbitrary repeatability of some elements, and special characters to represent a variety of languages, is outside of the mainstream of traditional data processing; even after many years, the intricacies of library practice have not yet entirely yielded to rigorous analysis.

Although these problems are particularly acute in Greece because of the general condition of librarianship there, they are by no means unique, and there is much that can be learned quickly from years of experience gained in other countries. Training abroad, international professional contacts, and increased access to a variety of on-line library systems through international telecommunications networks can make a tremendous difference in raising the level of consciousness in Greece with regard to library automation.

Lastly, it must be said that in spite of the risks of developing a system, there is much to recommend this approach. Even if the goals are limited or the product falls short of expectations, there is much to be gained in the process. System development can be a good way to gain valuable experience and insight while solving some immediate practical problems. Any plan should be flexible enough that it can be modified, or even abandoned, as circumstances dictate, without an excessive loss of resources; the likelihood of migration to a completely different system as new opportunities arise should also be taken for granted. It is also important to recognize that one of the greatest benefits of library automation is resource sharing. The ability to exchange bibliographic data among Greek libraries and with the international library community will be one of the most significant goals to work toward in the coming years.

Both of these considerations dictate that the representation of data needs to be given much thought and care. At the record level, it is important to preserve standard numbers such as ISBNs and Library of Congress Card Numbers. This will facilitate matching and merging of records from multiple databases, and will also make it easier to upgrade any substandard records created on systems with limited capabilities. At the character level, the system should be designed to store character values in such a way that they can be translated with minimal loss of data for the purposes of exchange with, or conversion to, other systems.

THE CHARACTER SET PROBLEM

The technical problem of library automation that sets Greece apart from other Western countries is the need to routinely handle both the Greek and Latin alphabets. There is a widespread dependence, particularly in some academic collections, on materials published in other Western European languages, and many Greeks have acquired a functional knowledge of one or more of them.

This multilingualism affects other aspects of Greek life as well, and different techniques have been used in the data processing industry to accommodate it. On earlier systems restricted to 7-bit character sets, the two alphabets could be used together only if they were both limited to upper-case letters. This appears to be the case in the system described by Papadoperakis. More common today are computers that have 8-bit character sets that include the complete basic Greek and Latin alphabets in upper- and lower-case, as well as additional compound characters with diacritics. The standard terminals used with this kind of system represent all or most characters of the modern Greek writing system, as well as those of the more common European languages that use the Latin alphabet. Although these terminals lack some obsolete Greek characters and diacritics, many of the extended Latin characters are included in the various national and international standards for bibliographic data.

Probably because these systems do such a good job of displaying bibliographic data in a variety of common languages, each library system developed thus far in Greece seems to accept the character set of the hardware being used as a standard, with little or no attention to existing standards for bibliographic data. The consequence is that any character not explicitly included in the local character set is compromised or lost, and any exchange of records between different systems is likely to result in degradation of the text, because of differences from manufacturer to manufacturer and even from model to model.

The solution to this problem is complicated by the fact that there is no single standard that should clearly be adopted. It is further complicated by the fact that librarians have developed their own character-set standards separately from the computing community at large. This unfortunate situation, and the various standards that have been developed at different levels, are discussed comprehensively by Clews.[8] Further insight into the politics of standards development–and some discussion of general principles of character-set implementation–is presented by Birnbaum in a paper that focuses on Cyrillic characters.[9]

Some of the relevant standards developed by the computing community are International Organization for Standardization (ISO) 646 (the international standard for the basic Latin, which corresponds to American Standard Code for Information Interchange (ASCII) in the U.S.) and ISO 8859, which includes four extended Latin sets and a modern Greek set (corresponding to ELOT 928, a Greek national standard). In the years to come, the character set capabilities of standard terminals and other equipment are likely to reflect these standards. ISO Technical Committee 46, representing the library community, has developed a number of character sets to supplement ISO 646, which have all been incorporated into the Universal Machine Readable Cataloging (UNIMARC) format. These include ISO 5426, an extended Latin character set that handles most Latin character-set languages and transliterations, and ISO 5428, a Greek set. ISO 5428 is fuller than any existing national Greek standard in that it includes the obsolete characters and diacritics needed to accommodate the orthographic conventions used for classical texts and more traditional forms of Modern Greek, as well as the simplified conventions now in use. Related to ISO 646 and 5426 are a number of national standards of varying compatibility, among them the USMARC character set. Some of these make their own provisions for coding Greek characters.

In the interests of international compatibility for the purposes of record exchange, it would make sense for Greek librarians to develop a national standard that includes the basic and extended Latin characters of ISO 646 and 5426, the Greek characters of ISO 5428,

64   ACADEMIC LIBRARIES IN GREECE

and perhaps some modifications or extensions to accommodate extra characters found in USMARC and other national standards. It remains to be seen, though, how long it will take to develop any kind of standard for a bibliographic character set in Greece, and how extensive a repertoire of characters Greek librarians can feel justified in supporting. The high degree of precision required to transcribe archaic and unfamiliar text using such full-character sets may seem irrelevant or unreasonable given the present realities. In practice, it is likely that in the immediate future databases will be created from various sources with different levels of character encoding; it might be useful to define a data element for bibliographic records to differentiate and specify these different levels.

However the issue is ultimately decided, it should not be done according to the simple convenience of adopting the character set of the hardware at the local site. Apart from the growing awareness of the various existing character-set standards, there is a more practical reason to hope that a broader approach to character representation will take hold. This is the increasing importance of networking in the computer industry and in the library world. Access to databases now routinely crosses both hardware boundaries and political boundaries, and it is impossible for simple methods of character representation to match the display and input requirements of all of a system's users. In spite of growing standardization–or perhaps because of the proliferation and sophistication of standards–this problem will be more apparent in the coming years, and it should influence system designers to adopt more complex character-mapping techniques that will serve a variety of needs.

In any case, the internal representation of bibliographic character data in a system should not be governed by purely local concerns, nor need it be subject to the inherent limitations of an 8-bit character set. A more general approach can accommodate both a large character set and the diversity of terminals and network connections, though it seems inevitable that some of the data must be represented in at least two different ways within the system. For input and storage, the representation may conform as much as possible to the native character set of the machine on which the database is stored, but any remaining unmapped characters should be represented by editable escape sequences. Indexes, on the other hand, should be built by normalizing the data to a limited set of basic characters. For display and entry of search terms, a variety of options should be provided; these options should be selectable by the user according to the type of terminal, the telecommunications link, and other special needs (e.g., the ability to edit). The software can be made to dynamically translate the data as it moves back and forth. Such a scheme complicates system design, but it accommodates the realities of networking and makes possible the large character sets needed to maintain data compatibility with other systems.

To illustrate the range of possibilities, catalogers need, at one extreme, to be able to view and edit each distinct character in the set as unambiguously and as conveniently as possible. At the other extreme, users on another continent with only a basic Latin character set on their terminal should be able to see a transliteration of any Greek text and enter Greek searches with Latin characters. Greek users on a network with a 7-bit telecommunications protocol should be able to see text in upper-case Latin and Greek characters, if their terminals are of this type. Scholars with an interest in classical texts or rare books, and a specialized PC character set, might prefer to see the archaic Greek orthography (albeit at the expense of some compromise in the display of special Latin characters). Most users would have standard terminals or PCs with extended character sets and would find that the vast majority of records, whether in Greek or other languages, would display correctly.

TRENDS

In closing, it seems appropriate to reflect briefly on library automation in the general context of Greek librarianship. Perhaps the best place to start is library education. Although the structure of library education is essentially the same as described by Krikelas in 1982 (two programs at the vocational-technical level, one in Athens and the other in Thessaloniki),[10] there has been a dramatic improvement in conditions, judging from contacts with the school at Thessaloniki. The faculty is dynamic and progressive, and there is evidence of a considerable investment in facilities in recent years, including a sizable computer lab and a growing library collection. A number of students serve a practicum in the Central Library of the

University of Thessaloniki, and more and more of them are being hired to work in the many libraries there. This is an encouraging trend, showing that the old staffing patterns documented by Krikelas (by which "one does not apply for a librarian's position as much as for a position within a governmental agency"[11]) are beginning to break down.

Another indication that the status of librarianship in the University is improving can be seen in the fact that many of the traditionally numerous, scattered collections with limited access are being consolidated at the departmental level. This is probably attributable both to changes in the law[12] and to the influence of faculty who have experienced high-quality library services while studying abroad[13] and who are now moving into positions of authority from which they can initiate reforms.

Finally, there seems to be a widespread consensus among librarians that automation has an important role in the development of libraries in Greece. The different independent projects that originally sprang up in isolation are becoming more widely known through personal contacts and conferences on library automation that have taken place in various parts of the country (Crete in 1988, Thessaloniki in 1989, and Athens in 1990). Most important of all is the fact that these projects are beginning to benefit and reinforce each other.

Thanks to the establishment of an X.25 data network by the Greek telephone company, the on-line databases created by the National Documentation Center are now available by dial access or dedicated line, at least in some parts of the country. The Center has also done some work on a simple cataloging program for libraries, and has distributed it widely. Some of the University computing centers, such as those at Crete and Thessaloniki, are nodes on EARN (the European counterpart of BITNET) and are now beginning to connect to the Internet. This has done a lot to improve communications among librarians in Greece and with colleagues in other countries; it has also made possible the cooperative activity between Thessaloniki and Crete.

The creation of an on-line national database is a vision that should inspire and guide library automation in Greece in the coming years. It holds out the promise of a revolution in access and service, and it provides a powerful motivation for a commitment to develop-

ing standards and other forms of cooperation. Given the achieve-
ments of the last few years (and prospects for further progress), it is
not an unreasonable goal.

REFERENCE NOTES

1. Pericles Papadoperakis, "The Automation Project at Library B of Thrace University," *Program* 16 (April 1982): 57-66.
2. James Krikelas, "Academic Libraries in Greece," *International Library Review* 16 (July 1984): 242.
3. Nancy Birk and Dimitris Karageorgiou, "Academic Libraries in Greece: A New Profile," *Libri* 38 (June 1988): 88.
4. C. Skourlas, "National Documentation Centre: Software Development for Public Databases Management," in *Online Information 88, 12th International Online Information Meeting, London, 6-8 December, 1988, Proceedings*, Volume 2 (Medford, NJ: Learned Information, 1988), pp. 629-640.
5. T. Alevizos, E. Galiotou, and C. Skourlas, "Information Retrieval and Greek-Latin Text," in *Online Information 88, 12th International Online Information Meeting, London, 6-8 December, 1988, Proceedings*, Volume 2 (Medford, NJ: Learned Information, 1988), pp. 791-802.
6. The term "Latin" is used here because it corresponds to Greek usage and seems more generally accepted internationally than "Roman," which is more common in the United States.
7. Aliki Tsoukala, personal communication, November 29, 1989.
8. John Clews, *Language Automation Worldwide: The Development of Character Set Standards* (Harrogate: Sesame Computer Projects, 1988).
9. David J. Birnbaum, "Issues in Developing International Standards for Encoding Non-Latin Alphabets," in *Proceedings of the Fourth International Conference on Symbolic and Logical Computing*, ed. Eric Johnson (Madison, South Dakota: Dakota State University, 1989), pp. 41-54. Also available on BITNET as the file ISO8859 CRITIQUE from the ISO8859 list at JHUVM.
10. James Krikelas, "Education for Librarianship in Greece," *Library Quarterly* 52 (July 1982): 231-232.
11. *Ibid.*, p. 236.
12. Birk and Karageorgiou, "Academic Libraries in Greece: A New Profile," p. 85.
13. Krikelas, "Education for Librarianship in Greece," p. 235.

Automation
of the National Library
# of Greece

George D. Bokos

This presentation of the issues and problems associated with the automation of the National Library of Greece (NLG) has the following objectives:

1. To give as clear and full a view as possible of the requirements that must be met to automate the NLG's operations and services in a comprehensive manner.

2. To outline in what ways and to what extent computers and automated procedures are being used today at the NLG; to explain the rationale for the adoption of the system being used; and to analyze its strong and weak points.

3. To sketch the possibilities and prospects that are opening up now in the face of a full assessment of the problem of automating the National Library of Greece.

THE AUTOMATION OF THE NLG:
ASSUMPTIONS AND REQUIREMENTS
FOR A COMPREHENSIVE SYSTEM

It must be clarified at the outset that the NLG is not an automated library. It is a library that has made some progress in using comput-

This paper was originally delivered at the Department of Library Science, Technical Education Institute, Thessaloniki, Greece, on November 29, 1989. It was translated into English by Michael Kreyche and Athena Salaba.

ers in some of its operations and is now looking for a comprehensive solution of its automation problem. Before any discussion of the assumptions and requirements to be met in automating the National Library, questions as to its necessity and feasibility must be answered. The need to study and answer these questions correctly, before taking any action, has been stressed over and over again in articles on library automation.

Such questions were, in fact, important in the early days of introducing automation into libraries, when relevant experience was nonexistent and hardware was very expensive. Today, the situation is different. There has been considerable experience; powerful and relatively cheap computers; proven software; and, finally, established international standards–Universal Machine Readable Cataloging e.g., (UNIMARC) and Common Communication Format (CCF). There is also the fact of the tremendous spread of automation in libraries, at least in Western countries. This is especially significant if we consider that the international context of our work as professional librarians has shown a tendency to radically change the methods and tools of our work, just as it tends to change the format, delivery, and use of data as well as the product of our work, information. A typical instance of this change is the movement from print to magnetic and optical media for storage and transfer of information (CD-ROM, for example).

It is consistent with this perspective that the discussion of problems relating to the introduction of automation into libraries, a discussion that has dominated professional journals and conferences in our field in recent years, has given way today to more highly specialized problems relating to new technologies in libraries (for example, the retrospective cataloging of old collections of library materials). Automation is seen as a reality in librarianship, and now it truly is. So, the question today is not so much whether a library needs to be automated or not. For a variety of reasons, it will be imperative at some point to proceed with automation in some form or other, and to make a fundamental change in the basic tools and methods of a library's work. The principal question is: How to automate?

This reality has taken hold to a very great degree at the National Library of Greece, the nation's central library, with its significant national and international obligations. There is no question today as to whether the National Library will be automated or not. If the Library's operations are not automated:

- It will not be in a position to cooperate and exchange data with other national libraries or other kinds of libraries and information centers, either at home or abroad. The European Economic Community (EEC), to which Greece belongs, will soon put into operation a special program for promoting the use of new technologies in the Community's libraries. An environment is being created and developed to which Greece must be careful to adapt in a timely manner, because otherwise it will be obliged to face a very painful isolation.

- It will not be in a position to use today's data to develop, at a reasonable cost and in harmony with current international plans, the basic services needed by our country. These include the publication of the National Bibliography and the creation of tools such as a union catalog of material in Greek libraries.

- It will not be in a position to use the modern information products available in our field, which will be produced with the use of new technologies and will depend on the new technologies for their delivery and manipulation.

The need, consequently, to proceed with the automation of the National Library is very compelling. However necessary the introduction of automation is, it is nonetheless difficult to know the right direction to move in. This difficulty, which holds true for every application of automation, is even truer for applications in libraries. And it holds especially true in the case of libraries such as our National Library, since the decisions and choices that are made must take into account the international view as well as the national reality. This problem is all the greater in Greece, because library automation has not yet gotten off to a solid start, and there is no fundamental work on which to build. So for the National Library to position itself for progress in automation, it must make decisions and proceed with choices that will not create problems but that on the contrary, will facilitate cooperation among Greek libraries.

On the other hand, the automation of a relatively large library like the NLG presents serious organizational problems, since it entails the replacement of one fairly complicated system with another. What is more, in the case of the NLG, any automation plan or program must provide for the development of a significant number of new functions and services that the library is not now in a position to offer. The problems that must therefore be solved are many and have as much to do with issues of general importance (for example, the format to be used for the entry of data elements into the computer) as with matters unique to the National Library. These problems clearly cannot be treated within the scope of this presentation. Worthy of mention here, however, are the more general requirements that the future automated system of the NLG must meet, considering that it must fulfill both the internal requirements of the library and its broader national and international obligations.

A comprehensive automated system for the NLG, regardless of the process and time frame of its realization, must at the very least meet the following requirements:

- Assure the integrated automation of the NLG on the basis of the creation of, and shared access to, a union bibliographic database.

- Have the capability–both in terms of its capacity to store and manipulate large files and in terms of its processing speed–to support the creation, management, and use of an electronic database of the National Bibliography of Greece.

- Offer the ability to network with other libraries to exchange bibliographic data and information services, both within and outside of Greece.

THE PRESENT SITUATION

What is described above constitutes the very generally formulated objectives and aspirations of the NLG with regard to the complete automation of its operations in the future. A question that eventually follows from the foregoing and that is appropriate to answer here is why the National Library has not yet managed to confront its automation problem as comprehensively as is necessary and desirable. The reasons are twofold:

1. The formidable bureaucracy and procedures established by the Greek Presidential Ministry to regulate requests and approvals for governmental agencies to obtain information products. These procedures have at times been justifiably scrutinized, since significant amounts have been spent on the procurement of computer systems without sufficient attention to appropriate issues, resulting in systems that have remained unutilized. But today, they constitute a significant restraint on similar efforts, even beyond the generalized problem of bureaucracy in Greece.

2. The more general difficulty that the introduction of automation in an actual workplace leads to. One must not forget that even today, with many years of experience, when the computer tends to be a tool in our daily lives, the introduction of automation is not an easy proposition. It means above all a general change in procedures, in workflow, and in the way we learn to work. It means also that we are obliged to familiarize ourselves with new tools that have a different logic and make different demands on their users. A hurried attempt to automate our work without the requisite preparation could lead to very serious, even catastrophic disorder. The larger the site where automation is being undertaken, and the more procedures involved, the greater the danger.

The National Library began to seriously address the problem of automating its operations in 1984. At that time, it became clear that the bureaucratic procedures involved in complete automation would be extremely time-consuming. It was also clear that the staff did not have the appropriate experience (and, of course, it was impossible to hire new staff). At the same time, it was clear that the nature and organization of the library's work, as well as the products it was obliged to deliver, resulted in a considerable duplication in the typing up of bibliographic data for the material brought into the library each year.

It was obvious that the use of a computer system would prove extremely useful for the library, since it would allow the library to make improved use of a significant number of workers, especially at a time when the ability to increase its very limited staff was, and would continue to be, nonexistent. The only kind of system that the NLG could move to at that time, without being subject to the time-consuming bureaucratic requirements of the Presidential Ministry, was one based on microcomputers, which were limited to addressing only the basic operations and needs of the library. The library decided to proceed immediately with this solution for the following reasons:

1. The installation of the system could be accomplished fairly quickly.
2. There would be a very significant gain for the library from freed-up workers.
3. It would have as a consequence the gradual familiarization of the staff with computers and their use in library applications.
4. It would offer the library the ability to build considerable experience in dealing with the problems of introducing and using computer systems.

At the same time, the NLG would be making a start in the process of moving toward a complete, integrated automation solution. The system that the NLG uses today serves the needs of, and generates products for, two of its departments: the Receiving Department and the Cataloging Department. According to the procedure that is followed, the material enters the Receiving Department, and when the necessary processing is completed there, it continues on its way to the Cataloging Department. In the Cataloging Department, it undergoes the next phase of processing in the Offices of Descriptive Cataloging, Subject Cataloging, and Classification. Through the course of the material's journey, each department and office contributes the data for which it is responsible.

The Receiving Department is responsible for assigning an accession number to every item and for determining the genre of Greek literary works. This latter task, somewhat strange for a receiving department, has to do with a special obligation of the National Library to prepare an annual catalog of the preceding year's literary works received by the Library. This catalog is used by a special committee of the Ministry of Culture to award annual literary prizes.

The Cataloging Department is responsible for the bibliographic description of the piece, for the subject headings assigned to its contents, and its classification number. When all the processing steps are completed, every piece (accompanied by a form on which all the above data are written) arrives in the data entry unit, where all the data are keyed into the computer once and for all. From this single entry of data for one item, the following products are printed in successive batches:

1. Cards for the library's public catalog. All cards appropriate to the catalog (authors, titles, subjects, etc.) are produced and ready to be sorted.
2. Labels with the call number of each piece, which are placed on the spine and cover.
3. The accession list of the library (legal deposits, gifts, and purchases).
4. The Receiving Department's annual catalog of literature, mentioned above.
5. The annual catalog of translations from foreign languages into Greek, a catalog that the library is also obliged to produce each year.
6. The semiannual issue and the annual volume of the Greek National Bibliography.
7. A catalog of multiple copies in the library.

With the use of this system, whose hardware and software costs at today's prices would not be more than Dr. 1,500,000, the NLG can free up about seven workers, the annual salary of each of them exceeding Dr. 2,500,000. Although this system has given the NLG the ability to save a very significant number of personnel hours, it nevertheless presents some serious disadvantages owing to the fact that its introduction was one of necessity rather than one that was properly devised and comprehensive. Specifically, the disadvantages are:

1. The system merely provides the printed products essential to the NLG, and is not able to offer other functions that might be expected of such a system (for example, information retrieval).

2. The system is used by only two of the units of the library and cannot be utilized by other departments for other purposes.
3. Files created are not compatible with the accepted international formats for entry and exchange of data, which means that it will be rather difficult to utilize them in the framework of future automation at the NLG.
4. The capabilities of the system do not allow the storage and management of a large number of files, and consequently do not allow the creation of a database that covers more than two years.

To address the problem of future utilization of the files being created–and to begin to create an electronic database of the Greek National Bibliography that can be manipulated in a variety of ways and can be made readily accessible to various categories of users– the NLG is proceeding with the adoption of the Integrated Set of Information Systems (ISIS) program, offered free of charge by UNESCO, which will be used mainly for the entry of data into the computer in the UNIMARC format. The resulting files will thus be completely compatible and can be manipulated and utilized in the context of the planned total automation of the NLG. It should be noted that these files are fully processible by the programs the NLG uses today in the preparation of the various products mentioned above and in its work with others.

Apart from the above system, which serves the cataloging and printing needs of the NLG, the Cataloging Department uses another distinct application for processing the subject headings that the library uses. For the creation of its subject catalog, the NLG uses Greek subject headings that are based for the most part on the equivalent Library of Congress Subject Headings, but with other appropriate aids, such as the Medical Subject Headings (MeSH). With these aids as a source, primarily for the cross references, the library creates and uses its own list of Greek subject headings.

For all the tasks related to production and management of this list, the Cataloging Department uses a special program that automates the whole procedure and so is indispensable for creating and using subject headings and cross references. The program provides the following functions:

- Entry of subject headings
- Verification of subject heading
- Deletion of subject headings
- Printing of cards for the subject division of the public catalog
- Printing, in book format, of the subject authority file
- Printing of supplements to the authority file

The use of this program enables the Department to control and manage a subject authority file that today has more than 20,000 headings. Something like this would have not been possible with the card method that was used previously, because of inconsistency in the use of terms and significant omissions in cross references.

PROSPECTS

What preoccupies the NLG now is the way in which it will proceed in the direction of total automation. Already, the library has approval from the Presidential Ministry and has begun work on an implementation plan, which is expected to be completed around the beginning of the year. Such a plan is not created to answer whether or not the National Library should be automated. But it must answer questions having to do with choices to be made, especially concerning the procedures and time frame for the introduction of automation.

The road to automation will not be easy, of course. And the difficulties are found chiefly in the weaknesses and problems of the library itself, as well as in the more general state of Greek librarianship. Much relevant experience has been gained, many of the problems are solved, and the economic difficulties of such an undertaking are not now as great as once they were. The problem being faced at this time is the lack of the infrastructure necessary to install such a system and put it into operation. In part, this situation is accounted for by the fact that the above-mentioned special EEC program finances a very great percentage (up to 70 percent) of the activities, which means that Greece could proceed with the introduction of new technologies at almost no cost. Whether we have the requisite infrastructure and position to propose suitable programs and secure funding for them are matters that at this moment may sadly not be the case.

AFTERWORD

(The following summary of progress made by the NLG since this paper was presented was made by Dr. Bokos in October 1990.)

During the last 12 months, the NLG has made considerable progress toward the introduction of automation. A special committee has been set up with the objective to handle all the relevant matters and supervise the whole project.

A detailed study of the exact characteristics and requirements to be met by an automated system for the NLG has been undertaken and carried out by a team of external experts, in close cooperation with the automation committee and other members of the Library's staff. On the basis of the results of this study, the NLG is now preparing a Request for Information document, which will outline the desirable system and contain brief information about the requirements to be met. This document will be sent to potential suppliers, both in Greece and abroad, asking them to indicate whether the system outlined and the requirements described could be met. This step is considered absolutely necessary, especially in regard to foreign suppliers of automated library systems, since special requirements (e.g., the Greek character set) should be met and extensive "tailoring" will be needed if such a system is to be used in the Greek environment.

The next step will probably be the preparation of a Request for Proposal containing detailed specification of the operational requirements of the system; this document will be sent to the identified potential suppliers. A formal invitation to tender is expected to be sent early next year [1991] to the suppliers selected during the previous stages.

In the meantime, the NLG has secured the necessary funds for the whole project from both the EEC and the Greek government. Another special project, which is to be funded mainly by the EEC, is expected to start in November 1990. The main objective of this project is the conversion of the bibliographic and authority records produced by the existing system of the Library to the UNIMARC format, so that they can be used in the context of the new automated system.

Collection Development
and Interlibrary Loan
in Greek Academic Libraries

Stella Korobili

The responsibility of the academic library is to balance the requirements of the university with the individual needs of the users. In other words, it should support teaching and, at the same time, encourage changes in the curriculum and promote research. However, the academic library in Greece is more nearly a passive than an active mediator between knowledge and users. Greek librarians do not discuss the matter of systematic book selection. Phrases like "building the collection" of a library or "managing the collection" are unknown to most librarians.

At the end of the twentieth century, while knowledge has become extremely complex and information is expanding, academic libraries in Greece still rely on a decentralized system. They do not know which library owns a specific item needed to meet a patron's request. Although most librarians have realized that resource sharing is the only way that academic libraries can fulfill the needs of the patrons and can stay abreast of the needs, there is no technical background to facilitate such activities.

The academic libraries I am referring to are both central libraries of a university and branch libraries of a school, a department, or a laboratory. In a survey conducted in 1990 by a group of three professors of the Library Science School, with my participation, four out of 59 libraries that responded to this survey are considered central: the central library of the University of Thessaloniki, the central library of the National Metsovion Polytechnic, the central library of the University of Ioannina, and the library of Aegean University. The first two were established before 1930, while the other two were founded more recently.

The largest of the four is the central library of the University of

Thessaloniki, with two million volumes and 3,400 serial titles. However, most users of the library do not bother to check the library's catalog, since they do not have much hope of finding what they are looking for. The oldest library is that of the National Metsovion Polytechnic, which was established in 1914. This is also considered a large library, since it has 200,000 volumes and 1,124 serial titles. The Central Library of the University of Ioannina is not a separate institution, but it belongs to the University and its role is to coordinate more or less the library system of the university. The last one has only 13,000 volumes and 297 serial titles. It was established five years ago, and serves a rather small university.

There is a branch library in the University of Thessaloniki, the Library of Classical Philology and Ancient History, that has 170,000 unduplicated volumes and 160 serial titles. As for the rest of the libraries, thirteen librarians that work in the equivalent libraries did not know the size of their collections. Seventeen libraries have up to 1,000 books. Fourteen of these have fewer than 15 serial titles, one has up to 50 serial titles and another has up to 100 serial titles. The collections of nine libraries consist of about 3,000 volumes. Three of them have up to 15 serial titles, two have up to 50 serial titles, three have up to 100 serial titles, and one has up to 150 serial titles. Eight libraries have up to 6,000 volumes. One of them has up to 15 serial titles, two have up to 50 serial titles, three have up to 100 serial titles, one has up to 150, and one has up to 200 serial titles. Three libraries have up to 10,000 volumes: two of them have 100 serial titles and one has almost 300 serial titles. Finally, four libraries have up to 20,000 volumes. Correspondingly, the same libraries have a good number of serial titles. One of these has up to 400 serial titles.

Volumes of Books		Titles of Periodicals	
17 libraries	1,000 books	19 libraries	15 titles
9	3,000	6	50
8	6,000	10	100
3	10,000	4	150
5	20,000	5	200
2	200,000	3	300
1	2,000,000	1	400
		1	1,500
		1	3,500

The two oldest libraries are the largest ones, but the libraries established between 1940-1960 cannot be considered large. Two libraries with rather good collections were established between 1960-1979, and four libraries that have good collections, either of books or periodicals, were established in the past decade.

Periodicals are necessary if scientists and researchers are to keep up with developments in their fields and with the new technology. But for researchers to have access to periodicals, every library should have a comprehensive collection of abstracting and indexing journals. Scientists in Greek academic libraries have to look through the whole selection of periodicals. Only 13 out of 48 libraries maintain a file of abstracting journals, and 24 have some indexing journals. The figures below show the type of reference materials in 48 Greek academic libraries:

	Libraries
Bibliographies	31
Biographies	15
Encyclopedias	24
Dictionaries	46
Documents	8
Atlases	11
Indexes	24
Abstracts	13

Only four libraries have all types of reference materials except atlases. Non-book materials are not included in most library collections. Academic libraries in Greece do not seem to be interested in incorporating new formats into their collections. "To serve its community, the library will develop, organize, and exploit collections of book and non-book material, primarily within subject areas covered by the college, but with regard also for items of fundamental importance in related areas, in order that the overall aspect of the collections may be coherent and well rounded."[1]

Greece is a developing country, and as a result it has not advanced technologically. The Greek language is not included in the languages of modern sciences and technology. It is therefore necessary that Greece use the scientific and technical information generated in developed countries. Almost all Greek academic libraries put special emphasis upon foreign titles. Seventy-six percent of libraries have more than 80 percent of their books in foreign languages. The rates are higher when we are dealing with periodicals. Eighty-seven percent of the libraries have more than 80 percent of their serial titles in foreign languages. The libraries that have a lower percentage of materials in foreign languages are those of the School of Law, the School of Education, and the Modern History School.

The library is gathering, processing, and disseminating information to all the potential users. However, Greek academic libraries have been designed primarily to meet the convenience of the staff. While in most developed countries the student is the heart of the academic library, in Greece most academic libraries do not circulate materials to students. Thirty-two libraries provide lending services to students, while the rest circulate the materials only to faculty or in some cases to graduate students.

Circulation should be determined by the size of the collection, the number of copies, and the number of users. However, there should not be any kind of discrimination. Students in most Greek academic libraries can use the books only in the reading-room and can borrow a book or a periodical only for a couple of hours to make photocopies. In 38 libraries, students have access to reference materials; in 49 libraries they have access to periodicals. Only 16 libraries lend materials to users that are neither faculty nor students in their departments, and 15 provide lending services to the administration.

Circulation data are very important in measuring library performance and planning for the future. Librarians should know whether their choices meet the demand of the users, or whether they provide books that are not used. However, only 15 out of 49 libraries keep circulation data. Whether some books are used or not, or how often a book is used has so far not been studied by Greek academic librarians.

In addition to lending materials, the library should plan to offer a series of other services to its users. Library services should have a significant effect on the education program. "Technology may change, books may go out of print, but one thing remains the same—

patrons continue to ask reference questions."[2] What kind of services are offered by librarians in Greek academic libraries?

Services to the Users	Number of Libraries
Answer specific questions	38
S.D.I. (Selective Dissemination of Information)	6
Prepare bibliographies	10
Circulate periodicals	21
Index periodicals	5
Translate documents	1
Photocopy articles	31

Historically, in academic libraries all over the world, the teaching faculty used to be responsible for book selection and for collection building in general. But during the 1960s, selection responsibility was handed over to librarians, who, with some help from the staff, were able to fill in the gaps. In Greece, the teaching faculty is still responsible for collection building. The argument is that they know the literature of their field better than any one else.

In 12 of the 55 libraries that responded to the question "Who is responsible for the selection of materials?" there is some involvement of the librarians in this process. Librarians select some general reference books. In 42 libraries, each professor decides what he/she needs for his/her class. In a few cases, there are committees that decide how to allocate the money for the materials, but usually librarians do not participate in these committees. Full-time faculty with the time to build a collection are rare. Of 55 libraries, only one has a full-time professor who works in the library.

Though it seems reasonable that the experts should select the books, in most cases this does not work. Some of the faculty are not interested in ordering books; others are more active and order, for the most part, books that concern their own narrow fields. One can easily realize the gaps and weaknesses that result from such lack of coordination. However, it is difficult for anybody to criticize the quality of collections, because it challenges the authority of the professors. Most faculty believe that collection development is their responsibility, and they do not like to share this responsibility. So, library collections reflect their interests rather than the needs of the.

library or the needs of the university as a whole. The teaching faculty know what their students need, but only the librarians actually know what the students use in the library.

Collection development involves much decision making. How do the faculty select materials? What are the criteria they use? What are the variables that affect their judgment in order to build their collections? Only four academic libraries have a written selection policy. "The primary objective of the collection development policy, therefore, is to unify or focus expression concerning the current state and future direction of the collection. If we are to determine how policy works and how to use policy for purposes of collection planning, we need first to understand its operation as a system of communication."[3] It is evident that setting guidelines for librarians or whoever is involved in the selection process is a necessity. Such guidelines should be based on the characteristics of the community the library serves. The analysis of the strengths and weaknesses of the collection is vital so that the librarians can plan for a sound collection that anticipates the users' present and future needs. Finally, a formal written collection policy will inform everybody about the goals of the library and will give a means to evaluate the library's activities.

The development of a collection includes concern for quality as well as quantity. The librarian is required to express his or her views on the quality of the collection. For the library to operate effectively, it needs to be continuously evaluated in terms of its resources and services. Although evaluation of the collection is an integral part of collection development, most of the academic librarians in Greece have no tools for evaluating their collections and services. The few evaluations that are carried out are impressionistic and subjective. They include shelf scanning and, in a few cases, list checking, but no attempt is made to ascertain whether the patron is satisfied or not.

The use of materials is an important criterion in evaluating collections. "Effective collection evaluation and management require a more thorough knowledge of the content of a library collection than simply the number of titles in specific call number categories."[4] Eighteen libraries evaluate their collections: three of them every year, two every two years, two every three to five years, and the rest occasionally. In evaluating their collections, four libraries out of eighteen use the checklist method, three of them evaluate their collections by comparing them with the collections of other libraries, one uses quantifiable standards, one uses the statistical method, and seven make use of what expertise is available.

Even fewer libraries weed their collections. If librarians do not weed obsolete materials, redundant books, books with out-of-date information, and figures that are not important clutter up on the shelves. Two libraries withdraw their older materials every year, one every three to five years, and five occasionally. Six of these libraries belong to the Humanities and Social Sciences. In contrast, the information of the "hard" sciences is changing continuously, and consequently libraries that belong to these schools should weed obsolete materials regularly.

Any university professor with a claim to scholarship is, of course, a user of the branch libraries and realizes the interdependence of these libraries. A medical library only partially meets the needs of the users, and this is also true of chemical libraries and others. An archaeologist needs to know about economics, social sciences, and anthropology. So the traditional collection of the archaeological library does not meet all the needs of archaeologists.

A basic assumption that can solve the problems of the branch libraries is that cooperation is essential. There is a need for both interinstitutional cooperation and cooperation on a national level. Because of shortage of funds, a branch library cannot usually build a collection that meets all the requirements of its users. The libraries are not usually in a position to choose from among a list of important works, but they have to decide which titles the library has funds to acquire. The "information explosion" continues, more and more scientific books and journals are being published, and the prices are increasing. Books are very expensive, and the price of scientific journals is even higher. "Academic libraries are no longer self-contained, self-sufficient units on local campuses but participate in a great variety of consortia to make information and documents available regionally, nationally and internationally."[5] Academic libraries in Greece should realize that they can never hope to reach a good level of collection development unless they cooperate.

On the other hand, there is no need for duplication among collections. Promoting and maintaining cooperation is vital to the future of libraries. Yet the majority of university libraries in Greece have not established interinstitutional cooperation. Only sixteen of the libraries mentioned borrow books from other libraries in Greece and eight from abroad.

Cooperation in the sharing of resources is very important. Such cooperation presupposes the organization of materials and the use of new technology. Cooperative efforts between libraries should end up in the establishment of a network. "The increasing number and cost of books, the tightening of acquisition budgets, and the widening scope of academic curricula are making the book acquisition process more difficult every year. The appropriate use of available technology and the full utilization of networks and other sharing arrangements will make this task less so."[6] I believe that it is possible to create such a network in the University of Thessaloniki if each library contributes its fair share to the effort. The materials that are for interlibrary loan should be identified. There should be a cooperative acquisition project. The libraries lacking significant resources should attempt to keep up with their users demands. Each member library of the system must be rich enough to add something. Interlibrary loan is not a panacea for all problems. Most requests should be satisfied by the local library itself. Libraries that belong to laboratories and small departments should merge or form larger units. The libraries should take advantage of the opportunities networking affords by automating their procedures.

As has been said before, the use of new technology is indispensable for better service to the users. It is obvious that academic libraries cannot cope any longer if they continue to use traditional work methods. However, automation in libraries is low on our lists of capital priorities. Eighteen libraries have automated their activities so far. Many of the faculty members prefer the traditional ways of gathering information. Some libraries are about to introduce on-line public-access catalogs, whereas others believe, for whatever reason, that users should not use the automated system. Automation in the libraries was initiated mainly by enthusiasm, and its success depends on individuals within the libraries. A question that faces librarians is whether to buy a system from abroad or to develop one in-house. If libraries decide on the latter, programming analysts and professional librarians should cooperate and work together in developing their product. There are actually no packaged systems on the market that can be installed in Greek libraries. So the usual practice in Greek libraries is for a programming analyst to develop a system that he/she believes is proper for libraries.

Most libraries do not provide access to computerized databases. Very few libraries have access to an information retrieval system, but even those that do fail to make full use of the system. Nor do library users have access to it. The Library of the University of Thessaloniki has access to the Online Computer Library Center (OCLC), but it should also use bibliographic databases like Educational Resources Information Center (ERIC). Cost is the main factor preventing this.

In conclusion, one can say that there is a general feeling that Greek academic libraries do not meet their users' needs. The libraries are held in low esteem and are little used. National planning is totally absent. There should be some changes in government policy, legislation, and economic allocation concerning academic libraries. If librarians do not take control of collection building, the future of academic libraries in Greece will be bleak. This is the right time to set objectives in terms of resources required to satisfy the demand for library services.

All academic libraries need a collection development program. Collection development should involve the combined efforts of library staff, administration, and faculty. Such a program should not only set out to satisfy current demands but also try to satisfy future needs. This will result in the proper growth of collections and a number of other worthwhile changes. The collection development policy is a means to set and systematize guidelines for collection building. Librarians should concentrate on the development of standard criteria for academic libraries and start using scientific methods of gathering information on what part of the collection is used and what is not. Collection-use studies and citation analysis are needed.

The task of providing access to materials through new technology has become urgent. "The emphasis in libraries is shifting from collections to access."[7] A library that has access to an information retrieval system can infinitely expand the resources of its collection.

The use of CD-ROM and on-line databases is a necessity. An automated circulation system will provide information on which books are not circulated, which are overused, which require more copies, and even which should be withdrawn.

Libraries should make every effort to provide a high percentage of the materials needed by their users and circulate all kinds of materials. Lending services are in fact the backbone of the services a library offers. "The bulk of the stock should be available for loan to staff and students, full-time and part-time, in quantities and for periods of time commensurate with their different needs. Lending policies should be generous and flexible."[8] Resource sharing is necessary in academic libraries. These should devote the bulk of their collections to the needs of the students, while research materials and other little-used materials should be shared among similar libraries.

The admission of Greece to the European Economic Community will bring fundamental changes to the universities, and libraries will change accordingly. There are many opportunities for the academic libraries to develop, but they will also face many difficulties. "To remain relevant to society, libraries must change and, if they cannot make the transition, they will soon be relegated to the function of archival storage–a place to go to seek knowledge of the past."[9] There are some academic libraries that have started planning for change, while others have yet to take the first step in this direction. New methods must be developed if the libraries are to confront the new realities of the day.

REFERENCE NOTES

1. *College Libraries: Guidelines for Professional Service and Resource Provision* (London: The Library Association, 1982), p. 16.

2. Gerald B. McCabe, ed., *The Smaller Academic Library: A Management Handbook* (New York: Greenwood Press, 1988), p. 245.

3. Ross Atkinson, "The Language of the Levels: Reflections on the Communication of Collection Development Policy," *College and Research Libraries* 47 (March 1986): 140.

4. Beth M. Paskoff and Anna H. Perrault, "A Tool for Comparative Collection Analysis: Conducting a Shelflist Sample to Construct a Collection Profile," *Library Resources and Technical Services* 34 (April 1990): 199-200.

5. A. Robert Rogers, "College and University Libraries," in *The Library in*

Society, ed. A. Robert Rogers and Kathryn McChesney (Littleton, Colorado: Libraries Unlimited, 1984), p. 95.
   6. Charles A. Gardner, "Book Selection Policies in the College Library: A Reappraisal," *College and Research Libraries* 46 (March 1985): 45.
   7. Barbara B. Moran, *Academic Libraries: The Changing Knowledge Centers of Colleges and Universities* (Washington, DC: Association for the Study of Higher Education, 1984), p. 61.
   8. *College Libraries: Guidelines for Professional Service and Resource Provision*, p. 24.
   9. Barbara B. Moran, *Academic Libraries: The Changing Knowledge Centers of Colleges and Universities*, p. 24.

BIBLIOGRAPHY

Atkinson, Ross. "The Language of the Levels: Reflections on the Communication of Collection Development Policy." *College and Research Libraries* 47 (March 1986): 140-149.
Clapp, Verner W. and Robert T. Jordan. "Quantitative Criteria for Adequacy of Academic Library Collections." *College and Research Libraries* 50 (March 1989): 154-163. [Reprinted from *College and Research Libraries*, September 1965.]
College Libraries: Guidelines for Professional Service and Resource Provision. 1982. London: The Library Association.
Dyson, Brian, ed. 1989. *The Modern Academic Library: Essays in Memory of Philip Larkin*. London: The Library Association.
Gardner, Charles A. "Book Selection Policies in the College Library: A Reappraisal." *College and Research Libraries* 46 (March 1985): 140-145.
Harloe, Bart. "Achieving Client-Centered Collection Development in Small and Medium-Sized Academic Libraries." *College and Research Libraries* 50 (May 1989): 344-353.
International Conference on Research Library Cooperation. 1987. New York: The Haworth Press.
McCabe, Gerard B., ed. 1988. *The Smaller Academic Library: A Management Handbook*. New York: Greenwood Press.
Moran, Barbara B. 1984. *Academic Libraries: The Changing Knowledge Centers of Colleges and Universities*. Washington, DC: Association for the Study of Higher Education.
Paskoff, Beth M. and Anna H. Perrault. "A Tool for Comparative Collection Analysis: Conducting a Shelflist Sample to Construct a Collection Profile." *Library Resources and Technical Services* 34 (April 1990): 199-215.
Roberts, Elizabeth P. "Cooperation, Collection Management, and Scientific Journals." *College and Research Libraries* 48 (May 1987): 247-251.
Rogers, A. Robert 1984. "College and University Libraries." *The Library in Society*, edited by A. Robert Rogers and Kathryn McChesney. Littleton, Colorado: Libraries Unlimited.

Schmidt, Karen A. "Education for Acquisitions: A History." *Library Resources and Technical Services* 34 (April 1990): 159-169.

Schwartz, Charles A. "Book Selection, Collection Development, and Bounded Rationality." *College and Research Libraries* 50 (May 1989): 328-343.

Stirling, John F. 1982. *University Librarianship*. London: The Library Association.

Thomas, Lawrence. "Tradition and Expertise in Academic Library Collection Development." *College and Research Libraries* 48 (November 1987): 487-493.

Thomas, Sarah E. "Collection Development at the Center for Research Libraries: Policy and Practice." *College and Research Libraries* 46 (May 1985): 230-235.

The American Center Library in Thessaloniki, Greece

Vicki Syroglou-Bouki

Our library is a unit of the American Center in Thessaloniki. The American Center, which is an overseas branch of the U.S. Information Agency (USIA), includes cultural affairs and press offices, as well as the library and an educational counseling service (part of the United States Educational Foundation in Greece).

The American Center Library of Thessaloniki, Greece, was established in 1949. Its purpose is to support the U.S. Information Agency's worldwide mission to "strengthen foreign understanding of American society, obtain greater support of U.S. policies, and increase understanding between the United States and other countries."[1] To achieve this goal, the U.S. Information Agency "engages in a wide variety of communication activities–from academic and cultural exchanges to press, radio, television, film, seminar, library, and cultural center programs abroad."[2]

The small lending library focuses on reference/referral and outreach services. It has a current collection of 6,000 volumes, 80 periodical subscriptions, and 300 videotape cassettes. In addition, the library provides the Thessaloniki library patron with computer-search services through our library in Athens.

The library program is handled by a staff of two librarians under the immediate supervision of the American Center Director, a U.S. foreign service officer. Continuous in-service training for the staff is provided. There are frequent visits by the Rome-based Regional Library Officer, and participation in continuing-education correspondence courses and exclusively designed seminars is encouraged.

Library users include university faculty and students, political personalities, members of the Greek Parliament, government and municipal officials, the city's civic, educational, and research institutions, professionals, artists, intellectuals, and the average Greek reader who loves the experience of an open-stack library.

This is neither an academic library nor a public or research library. It is a contemporary American library whose collection focuses on materials about the United States. The library also has a small reference center that offers Greek businesspersons information on U.S. manufacturers, exporters/importers, banks, economic theories, and current news on trade and business. At the same time, it provides the faculty and students of the Department of English Language and Literature of the University of Thessaloniki with literary criticism on the majority of classic and contemporary American authors, whose works are also available in the library. We locate information for Thessaloniki Law School lecturers, professors, and students on the U.S. Constitution, comparative constitutional law, U.S. history, law digests, treaties in force, international relations, foreign relations of the U.S., and biographies of prominent personalities in American politics.

In addition to our book collection, we keep a vertical file of leaflets, brochures, newspaper clippings, news cutouts, and flyers on a variety of issues. Examples of these holdings include material on the Conference on Security and Cooperation in Europe (CSCE); the Organization for Economic Cooperation and Development (OECD); the European Economic Community (EEC); the Food and Agriculture Organization (FAO); the General Agreement on Tariffs and Trade (GATT); space; the environment; drug abuse; terrorism; arms control; and disarmament and U.S.-Soviet bilateral issues. Our institutional program goals and audience preferences are our primary criteria for book selection and periodical subscriptions acquisition.

Besides lending books and periodicals and offering reference services, we promote library materials and usage through an outreach program. This program involves the publication of a monthly leaflet (one each for the fields of international affairs, economics, and the humanities), and we provide a limited TOC service for economics. We also disseminate pertinent information to important contacts in the political, academic, and business fields. The library supports all American Center cultural and press programs by issuing bibliographies on topics such as "Next Steps for NATO," "The Winning of the West," "Water Pollution," "Murals in America: The New Deal Era," "Labor and Laboring Classes in the U.S.," "Contemporary American Architecture," "Human Rights," "East-West Relations," and "The Soviet Union."

Greece is situated on the southern borders of the dramatically changing Balkans and Eastern Europe. A small U.S.-supported library in this part of the world plays a far greater role than meets the eye. Greek libraries lack a uniform cataloging system for their not-so-contemporary collections. This factor alone is a legitimate reason for the popularity of the library. An open-stack, Dewey-catalogued lending library like ours is, according to our patrons, an oasis in the desert. It is considered a "small library of substantial achievement." The Greek government-supported vocational School of Library Science considers our library to be a model library in this area of Greece.

REFERENCE NOTES

1. *The United States Government Manual* (Washington, DC: Office of Government Reports, 1988/89.)
2. Ibid.

Automation and the University of Crete

James Krikelas
Michael Tzekakis

INTRODUCTION

In a recent article, Hartley and Trohopoulos reported on visits to a group of Greek public and academic libraries. Their focus was on the current state of the use of information technology in Greece.[1] One of the institutions discussed–but not visited–was the University of Crete, which was characterized as "generally perceived as being the most advanced in the country."[2] Since little has been written about the University of Crete, this article provides a basic description of the development of the library and its automated system.

BACKGROUND

The University of Crete (UC) was established by national legislation in 1973 and began instruction during the 1977-78 academic year. The library of the university, however, was operational during the previous year, 1976. Prior to the commencement of instruction, the usual faculty and staff were assembled, but of particular significance was the early appointment of a librarian[3] who was given responsibility for creating a central library service. In a departure from previous policies, the university library is the principal agency for the purchase, processing, storage, and circulation of library materials. This is significantly different from the usual practice in Greece, where one finds small, independent collections under the control of faculty, with varying degrees of accessibility.[4] As Birk and Karageorgiou have noted, modern national legislation concerning academic libraries is still very scant; however, the current laws apparently discourage "small unit" collections and, instead, authorize the creation of central libraries–although departmental libraries are still allowed.[5] At the UC Library, every effort is made to achieve a high standard of library service, and this has led to a prominent degree of professional prestige within the University and among other Greek libraries as well.

As is the case with many Greek Universities of recent vintage, instruction is conducted in geographically distant campuses. The University of Crete operates in two separate cities on the island, Rethymnon and Iraklion, which are approximately 80 kilometers (50 miles) apart. An off-campus administration building for the university is located in downtown Rethymnon. There is also a research institute, the Foundation for Research and Technology (known by the initials ITE), that has a semi-official relationship with the university. Most of the research staff of the institute are also faculty members on their respective campuses. Four of the Foundation's research sections are housed in Iraklion and a fifth, the Institute for Mediterranean Studies, has offices in Rethymnon.

The Rethymnon campus houses the School of Philosophy (with departments of Philology, History and Archaeology, and Philosophy/Social Studies for secondary school teachers) and the School of Social Sciences (with departments of Economics, Sociology, and Psychology). There are also two Education departments for training Elementary School and Kindergarten Teachers. The Iraklion campus houses the science departments (Physics, Mathematics, Chemistry, Biology, and Computer Science) on the main campus and the Medical School at a different site. Approximately 2,700 students are enrolled on the Rethymnon campus, which has a teaching staff approaching 200. Over 1,700 students matriculated at the science campus in Iraklion, where there are approximately 120 faculty members. Current enrollment at the Medical School is 330; it has a faculty of 75.

THE LIBRARIES

Each site has a single library that is nominally under central administrative control from Rethymnon–although the Iraklion locations, because of their distance, are given a great degree of autonomy. The Rethymnon library contains 120,000 monographs, plus 25,000 bound periodicals. Current periodical subscriptions number approximately 850 titles, of which fewer than 175 are Greek-language publications. The Iraklion science campus library spends almost ninety-five percent of its annual acquisitions budget on 650 periodical titles covering the natural sciences. The total collection contains 26,000 monographs and 14,000 bound periodicals. The Medical School collection has approximately 8,000 monographs and bound periodicals, and it subscribes to 125 medical periodical titles annually. The collections are classified using the Library of Congress (LC) classification system. This decision, made during the early years of planning, permits the heavy use of external bibliographic sources to assist the staff in cataloging and classification. The choice, however, also creates some special problems for the Rethymnon campus, with its heavy emphasis on history and modern Greek literature, since the LC schedules in this area are woefully inadequate.

The Iraklion library has spacious quarters located within the main campus complex, which is a single, large multi-wing building that was built in 1979. The Rethymnon campus was originally housed in two existing buildings that had served previously as a technical school. As the needs of the campus–and the library–grew, two new buildings were constructed and additions were made to the two original buildings. The library moved into a laboratory room and later expanded into four adjacent rooms. Further space was acquired when a mezzanine was added to an existing sixth room. At the present time, the library has approximately 1300 square meters of floor space. Nevertheless, the consequence of this growth pattern is that the physical facilities–a series of connected individual rooms–present a challenge for providing modern library services. The problem will be partially alleviated with a new library; a new campus is currently under construction at a different site, some 10 kilometers west of the current location.

As would be expected, the focus of the Iraklion library's collection development policy is on current information in the sciences. This explains the heavy dependence on periodical literature; all of the periodicals are in non-Greek-languages. The predominance of non-Greek-language materials is also characteristic of the monographic collection. The situation is different in Rethymnon, where there is a heavy emphasis on Greek history, Greek and Mediterranean archaeology, modern Greek literature, Greek theater and drama, and Greek musicology. The collection consists of approximately 55 percent of Greek-language materials; the remaining 45 percent are in various foreign languages. The collection has been strengthened by the purchase or donation of a number of significant private collections. Eleven different and outstanding private libraries numbering over 27,500 volumes have been donated to the university. In addition, over 10,000 volumes were added through the purchase of five other significant private collections. Of particular importance was the acquisition of the private libraries of the Cretan author Pantelis Prevelakis and scholars George Arvanitides, Angelos Papakostas, R. de Simony and Melpos, and Octave Merlier.

While the UC Library enjoys strong support from the university administration and faculty, it also suffers from a problem characteristic of Greece–insufficient staff. The Iraklion campus has a staff of nine librarians, plus a few hours of part-time and student help. In addition, there are two staff members located at the Medical library. At Rethymnon, there are ten full-time librarians, including the director. In addition, two temporary part-time staff have been employed, but only a limited number of student assistants are provided. The size of the staff is even less adequate than appears at first glance because the library remains open for unusually long hours, compared with traditional Greek academic library standards. The library in Rethymnon, for example, is open daily from 9 a.m. to 8 p.m. and from 9 a.m. to 2 p.m. on Saturday. Staff members, however, normally begin work at 7:00 a.m. and, through a rotation system, at least one or more work until 9:00 p.m. All this must be achieved within an average 35-hour work week.

Technically, the Rethymnon library has no clerical help. All staff are considered to be filling professional positions, although many of them have no formal library instruction, outside of on-the-job training. To compound the problem of limited staff at the two main sites, maternity leaves of four months are provided for the female staff without any temporary replacement being budgeted. Furthermore, the normal work week of 37 1/2 hours is reduced for women with small children: by ten hours a week for those with children under two and by five hours for those with children under four. While the liberal Greek policy concerning maternity leave is commendable, the failure to incorporate temporary replacements constitutes a hardship on the remaining staff. In Rethymnon, for example, eight of the nine staff members–outside of the director–are women.

Given the constraints of limited staff, the library on each campus endeavors to provide more than a book-storage service. On the Rethymnon campus, direct user assistance is provided by a reference librarian who is on duty from opening hours until 2:00 p.m. and by the serials librarian from 2:00 p.m. until closing. Additionally, one member of the staff works in the library on Saturday, thus ensuring some knowledgeable assistance is available to the user. Some measure of the amount of activity in Rethymnon is reflected by the average yearly acquisition of 4,000 titles and by the 25,830 items circulated during the 1989-90 academic year. (Current circulation figures for September through March indicate that that total will be surpassed, even though there was a student strike in January.)

AUTOMATION: PHASE I

Library automation was developed at the University of Crete beginning in 1986. At that time, a substantial amount of funding was earmarked for the conversion of the library's operations from a manual to a computer-based system. Since the Rethymnon campus did not possess a computer at the time, the work was done at the Iraklion campus' Computing Center. The programs were written using SQL/DS software running on one of the Center's two IBM 4361 computers.[6] Early in the developmental stages, it was found desirable to move the programs to a more generic database management system. After some investigation, it was decided to rewrite the programs–with modification–to run under the INGRES information system. Thus, even before completion of the initial task, modifications that affected the scope of the project were contemplated. In accordance with this general decision, a Digital Equipment Corporation VAX (model 3400) was purchased and installed on the Rethymnon campus for future use. Only three IBM terminals were acquired for use on the Rethymnon campus (via dedicated lines to Iraklion), which resulted in limiting the activities that could be accomplished effectively. The two campuses, therefore, operate in different modes in the current IBM-based configuration.

The initial planning called for the development of a cataloging production system, a barcode-based circulation system, and an on-line public-access catalog (OPAC). As part of the original plan, it was determined that the systems would be Machine Readable Cataloging (MARC)-compatible (i.e., input and output would support the published MARC standards). (Cataloging adheres to Anglo-American Cataloging Rules, second edition (AACR2) standards.) To establish a workable database, arrangements were made to acquire machine-readable cataloging from a variety of external sources: the United States Library of Congress (LC), Baker and Taylor (book wholesalers with offices in the U.S.), and from Blackwell/North America (another U.S.-based jobber). Subsequently, additional records were acquired from the OCLC Online Computer Library Center (OCLC) via its European office.

The equipment limitations and the distinctive characteristics of the two collections led to a difference in activities between the two campuses. In Iraklion, the small book collection consisted primarily of foreign language materials for which existing MARC records could be purchased. The database was quickly built, and the testing of the circulation system was undertaken by mid-1990. At the same time, four OPAC terminals were installed and the on-line catalog module also became operational. The current barcode circulation system, of necessity, is relatively limited. All materials that can be borrowed have been marked with a locally generated barcode, and each user has been provided with a barcode identification card. A normal transaction permits the scanning of book and borrower data and the creation of a loan record; a date due is manually stamped in the book. Currently, the system also provides for "holds" on circulated books that have been requested by other users and for a daily batch-mode printout of overdue books.

The menu-driven on-line catalog requires the use of search keys (a specified number of characters from significant words) for title (3,2,2,1), author-title (4,3), and author (4,3,1) searches. An author-search request leads to a secondary menu that permits searches either by personal name, corporate name, or conference name. The system allows subject searches (also using a 4,3,1 key) as well as searches by four different numeric codes (accession number, LC card number, ISBN, and internal control number). On-line instructions in Greek are provided for users, although all examples are of English-language materials.

Systems responses are dependent on the access method used (author, title, author-title, etc.) and the number of "hits." Generally, the resulting screen is a list of line entries for each match; the display contains a line number, brief bibliographic data (author or title or author short title), and number of copies. A third menu level provides a screen showing brief bibliographic information (author, title, imprint); classification number; accession number; lending information (circulation, non-circulating, short-loan collection, normal); and location (main library, special collections, etc.). Catalog users may also request a fuller bibliographic record, which adds physical description, series entries, notes, subject headings, LC card number, ISBN, and control number. A printed brochure and on-line help screens are provided as aids to OPAC users.

The catalog data-input program, also a local product, is a menu-driven system as well. Catalogers may choose to call up a blank input screen or they may retrieve previously entered data. In the current version, the request for a work form results in the display of a two-part screen. The upper portion, similar in appearance to an OCLC screen, permits entry of information such as record status, record type, encoding level, language, dates, etc. The cataloger, however, is required to enter field labels, indicator codes and sub-field codes for each bibliographic element. (This has been changed in the new version.) To assist catalogers in the data-entry process, an on-line help screen offers a comprehensive summary of the MARC format information that may be required. The first of the multi-paged screen, for example, provides the relevant codes for the record status, type of record, encoding level, illustration code, and descriptive cataloging form; remaining screens cover all fields through the 700s. The keyboard permits toggling between Greek and Latin character sets within a field, allowing both character sets to be used in a single record. Upon completion of the MARC format data entry, and after saving the record, a holding screen can be called directly (via a PF key), thus permitting the addition of local holdings information. The holding screen permits the entry of an accession number as well as volume, part, and copy information. Retrieving a record for editing requires knowing one of four numeric values: the accession number, the Library of Congress card number, the UC record control number, or the ISBN. (This somewhat awkward step has been modified in the revised program, and access will also be possible by author, title, series, or keyword for record editing.)

At Rethymnon, two factors influenced the degree to which these programs could be implemented. The book collection, significantly larger, also contained a larger proportion (approximately 55 percent) of Greek-language materials. This represented a serious problem for two reasons: (1) the number of Greek-language materials that appear in external databases is relatively small and (2) the records that do exist in such databases are primarily stored in transliterated (Latin alphabet) form rather than in the vernacular. Thus, a substantial portion of work would require original cataloging. The approach followed, therefore, was to begin using the cataloging input system to record the Greek-language holdings. This process was aided by a parallel development.

In 1988, prior to the development of the automation project, the library joined with a British library in a research project sponsored by the Commission of the European Community (EC). The British library partner was King's College, London, and the objective of the project was to test the feasibility of cooperative conversion of Greek-language materials. The concept was a solid one, since King's College is purported to have one of the largest collections of Greek-language materials in Europe (outside of Greece). The project served as an excellent opportunity to train the Greek library staff in the use of MARC in a computerized environment; four Rethymnon staff members made brief working visits to London as part of the project. Equally beneficial, but on a slightly less positive note, was the recognition that using external sources would be extremely difficult for various reasons. Converting transliterated records (i.e., Greek materials represented in the Latin alphabet) back into Greek script proved elusive. The effects of different transliteration schemes also caused difficulties, as did other factors relating to language and script.[9] It was clear from this experience that much more original cataloging would be necessary and that the availability of the catalog production system in 1990 was fortuitous. Within the year, almost 5,000 of the 35,000 OPAC records created at Rethymnon were for Greek-language holdings in the two campus libraries.

By September 1990, three main components of the IBM-based system were operational: the circulation system using barcodes and light pen for the science library in Iraklion; the cataloging input system available to both campuses; and the on-line public-access catalog (OPAC) available to staff and public at Iraklion and to the staff at Rethymnon. Since a shortage of equipment (i.e., terminals) meant the OPAC was not available to library users in Rethymnon, catalog card production was required. A batch catalog printing program was developed as a supplement to the cataloging (input) program and card sets are printed on-site in Rethymnon. The printing program is capable of handling mixed Greek and Latin script and produces a traditional printed card format. The computer center staff created the programs that permit MARC tape input and MARC formatted output. A special tape conversion program (from United States Machine Readable Cataloging (USMARC) to United Kingdom Machine Readable Cataloging (UKMARC) was also created and tested as part of the EC project.

AUTOMATION: PHASE II

In late summer 1990, planning began on the rewriting of programs to run within the INGRES environment, thus making this a less machine-dependent program. At the same time, input was solicited to determine what changes might be useful in the existing programs and what other library operations should be added. Based upon this preliminary work, a tentative outline was developed: (1) convert the on-line catalog into a keyword-based system (thus eliminating the limits of search keys); (2) enlarge the circulation system to permit a broader range of traditional activities (blocks, reports); and (3) add a serials control component and an acquisitions module to the package. Initial programming began in late 1990, and a first-version test module of the on-line catalog and the new catalog input program were loaded in Rethymnon at the end of March 1991. A preliminary examination of the on-line catalog and the cataloging input program are in progress at the time of this writing.

The test version of the INGRES-based OPAC provides access via exact author, title, series, and subject entries, plus keyword access to the same fields. The system also permits truncated (or "wild-card") searches and the ability to delimit fields to be searched in the keyword mode. Thus, a typical exact author search is conducted by entering a phrase like the following:

AU = LAN, DAVID

a truncated search as:

AU = LAN%

while a keyword approach might appear as:

K = LAN DAVID.AU.

in which the keyword LAN and the keyword DAVID must occur in the author field for a match. At the present time, only the Boolean "and" is supported, although the "or" programming component is under development. Keyword searches may be general or limited to one or more of the indexed fields: author (1xx and 7xx), title, series (4xx and 8xx), and subject. The system also permits access by ISBN, Library of Congress card number, and system control number. Concurrently, the computer center staff continues work on the expanded circulation program and the new serials control and acquisitions modules.

CONCLUSION

Automating libraries is never an easy task; and in Greece, additional problems further complicate the procedure. There is no Greek equivalent to the Library of Congress or the British Library. Therefore, each institution works in isolation. Additionally, few commercial firms have ventured into the Greek library market because it is so small. Greek libraries must therefore deal with external agencies in the face of a relatively weak currency. Further, dealing with materials in two different scripts also presents numerous and costly problems. The dearth of sufficient, trained library personnel is another crucial issue that each library faces; progress in automation must also be viewed in this context. The steps taken at the University of Crete within the past three years, therefore, bode well not only for the university but for all Greek libraries as well.

REFERENCE NOTES

1. R. J. Hartley and I. Trohopoulos, "Information Technology in Greek Libraries: Problems and Prospects," *Program* 24 (October 1990): 333-342.
2. Ibid., p. 337, citing N. Birk and D. Karageorgiou, "Academic Libraries in Greece: A New Profile," *Libri* 38 (No. 2, 1988): 81-93.
3. The librarian, Michael (Mihalis) Tzekakis, had worked previously in the Rethymnon Public Library and is a graduate of the North London Polytechnic library school.
4. James Krikelas, "Academic Libraries in Greece," *International Library Review* 16 (No. 3, 1984): 235-246.
5. Birk and Karageorgiou, pp. 89-90.
6. The programming began, and continues, under the supervision of Grigoris Tzanodaskalakis, director of the Applications Program Section of the Computing Center.
7. For a brief description of the early stages of the EC project and the associated difficulties, see Evelyn Cornell, "Greek, Computers and Libraries," *Library Review* 38 (No. 5, 1989): 7-13.

Academic Libraries in Transition: A Case Study of the Library at the University of Crete in Rethymnon

Peter D. Haikalis

INTRODUCTION

During the Spring of 1989, I spent three months at the University of Crete in Rethymnon (UCR) on a Fulbright grant. The purpose of my assignment was twofold: to serve as a general consultant to the university library and to study how academic libraries in Greece function–their purpose, operations, and prospects for future development. In addition to my own observations growing out of that Fulbright experience in Crete, this article is based on conversations with professional colleagues in Greece as well as visits to university and research libraries in Athens, Thessaloniki, and at the TEI (*Teknologiko Ekpedeftiko Idrima*) located outside of Thessaloniki. Several of these pre-baccalaureate institutions have been established to prepare individuals in three-year programs for service in a number of fields: librarianship, teacher training, social work, agronomy, etc. Two of these TEI's, in Athens and Thessaloniki, offer librarian training. During my visit to the Thessaloniki TEI, I not only had the opportunity to meet and talk with the faculty at length but I was also privileged to lead a seminar attended by some sixty students.

BACKGROUND

Although libraries flourished in the classical era and during the thousand years of the Byzantine Empire, more recent times have not been as kind in providing a nurturing environment for such institutions. Political instability and economic hardship were the lot of Greece during the some 400 years of Ottoman rule, after independence, and even into the twentieth century. Many of the library resources gathered in earlier times were destroyed or dispersed throughout Europe. In Greece, after the fall of the Byzantine Empire, few collections of books existed outside of monasteries and the secret schools maintained by the Greek Orthodox Church. Opportunities for higher education were consequently limited for the most part to those who were able to leave the country.

Once independence was gained in 1827, the rebuilding of the country's library system was begun with the establishment of the National Library of Greece in 1829 and the founding of the library at the University of Athens in 1838. The university collections were soon merged with those of the National Library, which since that time has served as the library for the University of Athens. In 1845, a second major research collection was begun with the creation of the Library of Parliament. In 1925, the establishment of the Aristotelian University of Thessaloniki provided the opportunity for building a third major research collection. However, it was only after World War II, with the opening of universities in other parts of the country–Patras (1964), Ioannina (1964), Thraki (1973), Crete (1973), the Aegean Islands (1984), the Ionion Islands (1984), and Thessalia (1984)–that a system of academic libraries began to develop.

For the most part, the system of higher education in Greece was initially modeled on that of France and Germany. Even today, the influence of that early nineteenth-century European academic tradition remains. It can be seen in a highly autonomous faculty and structure of university governance; a strong emphasis at the undergraduate level on rote learning, with limited opportunities for independent study and research; examinations based on content memorized from formalized reading lists and lecture notes; a tendency at some universities for fragmented library collections housed in seminar rooms rather than open-stack, centralized facilities; and a disproportionately strong faculty voice in the allocation of financial resources for the acquisition of materials and provision of library services.

Given the environment of strong faculty prerogatives, a chronic shortage of funds, and a small pool of professionally trained librarians, academic libraries in general have had a difficult time establishing themselves as integral to the process of higher education. However, the libraries at the newer universities have begun to be recognized as full participants in the process, perhaps because these institutions are less influenced by traditions of the past. Many of the faculty members at the newer universities have been educated abroad, are accustomed to an academic environment with full-service libraries, and want similar facilities to support the local curriculum and their own research interests. The libraries at the University of Crete have been especially successful in articulating the library's mission in the overall context of the institution's educational endeavor and in gaining faculty support in pursuing it. Given the advances that have been made, Crete may well serve as a role model for its sister institutions and the library community as a whole.

THE UNIVERSITY OF CRETE LIBRARIES: AN OVERVIEW

The University of Crete was created in 1973, when the Philosophy School representing disciplines typically a part of the arts and humanities and the social and behavioral sciences was opened in Rethymnon (UCR). In Iraklion, Crete's largest city, a second campus of the University (UCI), housing the Schools of Pure and Applied Sciences and the Health Sciences, was established in 1979. During the initial stages of development, much of the university's business was conducted from Athens. Now the administrative center for both campuses is centralized and located in Rethymnon. The two towns are some 60 miles apart. It is less than a two-hour drive on a very good road, and as the telecommunications infrastructure improves in Crete the two campuses will become well connected electronically.

The University itself enjoys a good reputation throughout Greece, enrolling students from all parts of the country. The faculty is well trained and nationally recognized for its scholarship and teaching abilities. A substantial number of faculty members have done graduate work abroad, especially in the United States and England. At both campuses, the lecture and memorization mode of instruction is used less frequently as a means of instruction than at the older urban universities in Athens and Thessaloniki. Traditional teaching methods have been replaced by a less rigid and more research-oriented approach, with increased opportunities for independent and interdisciplinary study. This shift in the instructional mode, which requires strong library support and better access to library materials, tends to favor the establishment of a centralized, open-stack facility rather than the fragmented collections and the restrictive and often ad hoc practices characteristic of departmental reading rooms. This has been the case at both Rethymnon and Iraklion campuses.

At Iraklion, the university campus is located in a series of interconnected buildings of simple but modern design. The buildings have a high-tech appearance and are well furnished and maintained; the physical environment is functional and attractive. The library occupies a large space in the center of the complex. It is an open-stack, well-lighted facility with substantial study and work space. Although there is currently sufficient space for its holdings–some 25,000 books and approximately 600 periodical titles–there is concern about space for future growth. This facility serves as the central library for the Iraklion campus. Despite some demand to move in the direction of decentralized, departmental reading rooms, there has been sufficient faculty support to maintain the present system of housing all of the university's library collections together. With the completion of a new medical school center and teaching hospital across town, the health science materials will be transferred to the new site. Unfortunately, since there was little consultation with the library director or staff during planning of the new facility, it is unclear how space requirements for a collection and the supporting services for a library will be accommodated. What is undeniable is that there will be considerable disruption in service when relocation occurs. Physical separation of the two collections may spur efforts on the part of faculty members favoring departmental collections. However, at present those individuals, though vocal, seem to be in the minority. In the not too distant future, there will also have to be a major expansion of the present campus, and it is hoped that there will be closer and more appropriate consultation at that point in planning for additional library facilities.

At Rethymnon, the university is currently housed in temporary buildings on what was formerly the site of a technical high school. An elementary and middle school also share this space. The current arrangement is less than ideal, because of overcrowding and the close proximity of two very different student populations. Since this was intended as only a temporary location for the university, little money has been allocated for anything beyond basic, general maintenance. The site itself is unkempt, many exterior building walls are covered with graffiti, and the overall atmosphere of the place is somewhat depressing. Although plans call for the creation of a campus in the foothills to the south of town, political uncertainties and financial difficulties have postponed the full realization of this project. It was only a few years ago that work began on the Humanities Complex. This architecturally striking facility is nearing completion, and preliminary planning has now begun for several other large buildings, including a large space reserved for the university library. However, it is unclear, because of financial constraints and disagreements among university faculty and administration on matters of design, when the remaining buildings will be completed. Although the space assigned to the library in the present setting is itself less than ideal (i.e., fragmented, poorly ventilated and lighted, and not well furnished), the collections are substantial, comprising some 125,000 volumes, and are fully accessible in open-stack areas for use by faculty and students. In 1989, a two-story annex was completed that will increase the library's size by about 20 percent. This new addition will provide for better organization of the collection and also finally permit a sufficient work area for staff. However, it is anticipated that the overcrowding of collections, users, and staff will again become a major concern in the near future.

COLLECTIONS

When the libraries at the two campuses were established, considerable effort was expended in acquiring materials to support the initial curricular offerings and research interests of the faculty. At present, collections at the two campuses number more than 150,000 books and 2,000 journal titles. At UCI, about 90 percent of the materials are in English. At UCR, the collection is about 60 percent in Greek and approximately 30 percent in English, with mainly French and German titles making up the balance. Since textbooks are provided free to students by the state, both libraries also have substantial textbook collections as well. Unfortunately, the recent upsurge in rates for periodical subscriptions, particularly for technical and scientific titles, has begun to take its toll on the library collections. Monographs in the science collections at Iraklio are becoming dated and need to be replaced. For example, last year fewer than fifty new titles in physics were purchased. As is the case with libraries everywhere, price increases have necessitated making some hard choices about where to cut back–current periodical subscriptions or monographs acquisition–and, unfortunately, some of these decisions have not been made in the most objective manner.

The UCR collections supporting art history, philosophy, the classics, and modern Greek history and literature are strong. However, the core monographic titles, periodicals, and reference materials for disciplines more recently added to the curriculum (i.e., economics, psychology, and sociology) are not as good, since programs in these areas were initiated without adequate consultation about requisite library resources. The result is that there has not been sufficient economic support to ensure that each of the newer disciplines is supported by a good basic collection. Funding for all phases of the library program, including acquisitions, is done at the local level, and no clear-cut formula is available to provide guidelines about how much of the monies made available to the university by the state are allocated to the library. The matter appears to be settled by negotiation each year.

In addition to the aforementioned resources, there is a large quantity of books, pamphlets, and manuscripts at UCR that have not been cataloged. Action in processing these has been deferred in part because of lack of staff and because of continuing discussions regarding national cataloging and classification standards for Greek-language materials. Part of this material, which is primarily related to the history, literature, and culture of Crete, is printed on paper of poor quality, so preservation is a concern. In order not to lose the more fragile items, library staff have begun a systematic program of photocopying. The library has also arranged for off-site storage in order to provide a better physical environment for these materials. An ad hoc short-title listing of these items is also being developed. Realistically, this is about all that can be done now, given the lack of funds for processing and preservation.

At both UCI and UCR, the faculty has taken the lead in collection development and suggests most of the new titles for purchase. This is the traditional way that collections have been built, since qualified librarian bibliographers until recently have been virtually nonexistent. Faculty orders are processed as long as funds are available, and few if any requests are turned back as inappropriate. In many cases, faculty members engaged in the selection process have been extremely knowledgeable about publications in their field and have tried to ensure a broad and representative collection. However, the danger in permitting faculty such latitude in fashioning the collection is the potential for making choices that tend to reflect their own personal research interests and language preferences rather than what might be best for the program as a whole. In times of retrenchment or redistribution of resources, such reliance on faculty to shape the collection increases the risk of imbalance.

Collection development policy statements are not well developed, and few criteria are articulated regarding the scope and levels of materials to be acquired. Nor are there any guidelines available to help establish book-fund allocations. The library director and staff are well aware of the problem, and initial steps are being taken to correct it. The first steps in a collection analysis project were undertaken under my direction during my Fulbright tour. A title and volume count of monographs by the first two letters of their LC classes was completed. It is hoped that such an analysis will be valuable in resource allocation. In addition, library staff members possessing subject background by virtue of their baccalaureates have been assigned responsibility for processing and monitoring collections in their areas of competence. This is seen as an initial step in building a group of librarian bibliographers. As these individuals gain experience and expertise, it is hoped that they will earn the respect of faculty and be permitted to work more closely with them in a team approach to the selection process. Although the process will be a lengthy one, a cautious approach to cooperative book selection, an area that has traditionally been considered a faculty prerogative, seems well advised.

BIBLIOGRAPHIC CONTROL

Soon after the establishment of the two libraries, Michael Tzekakis, Director for both the UCR and UCI Libraries, adopted the Library of Congress Subject Headings and the Library of Congress Classification System for all books written in languages other than Greek. As a result, the card catalogs for non-Greek materials are organized in standard fashion, with access points similar to those we would find in libraries here. Card sets for English-language books were initially produced in house, but now are ordered from Blackwell whenever possible. Since commercially produced card sets have not been available for many of the art, history, philosophy, and philology titles, local cataloging and production of card sets have been major tasks for the UCR library. The process has been slow and tedious, resulting in a backlog of uncataloged materials. Adding to the complexity of the situation was a lack of permanent staff members, other than Director Tzekakis, who were formally trained in cataloging procedures. Thus, on-the-job training, with only the most basic cataloging reference sources available, has been the norm. This has been a herculean task, and the library director and his staff must be admired for persisting in this effort despite great handicaps.

At present, none of the Greek-language materials have been fully cataloged at either UCR or UCI. At Iraklio, this does not pose a major problem since the number of Greek-language scientific titles is limited. At UCR, however, the situation is exaggerated since more than half of the collection consists of materials written in Greek. At present, the only public access to the Greek collections is through brief title and author catalogs. There is no subject access. The materials themselves are arranged on the shelves in two major divisions–belle lettres and history and other non-fiction–then according to a code based on the first two letters of the author's last name, and finally alphabetically by title. As a temporary measure, this scheme is workable. However, it becomes increasingly cumbersome and ineffective as the collection grows. The reasons for such limited access are twofold: the lack of trained cataloging staff and the absence of nationally developed guidelines for the cataloging and classification of Greek materials. In the hope that national standards will soon be agreed upon by the Greek academic and research library community, it has been decided not to commit the library's very limited personnel resources to any further local cataloging. In one of the following sections of this article, the lack of progress in developing national standards is discussed in greater detail.

At Iraklion, the task of bibliographic control has been somewhat less difficult, since conditions there have been more favorable right from the time the library opened. Among these is the fact that one staff member, an American-trained librarian who worked as a cataloger in the United States before moving to Greece, was able to put her expertise to good advantage at UCI. Moreover, the UCI collection is smaller and consists primarily of English-language scientific material published since 1960, for which commercially produced card sets usually have been available. Several years ago, the university computer center, located on the Iraklion campus, became interested in developing a prototype for an on-line catalog and automated circulation system and has had considerable success with the project. All of the non-Greek-language materials in the UCI collection have been entered into the on-line file, and new titles are added as they are processed. Card sets have been generated by computer for incorporation into a card catalog, and it is hoped that the on-line catalog will soon be up and running. Plans have been developed to link the UCR and UCI libraries by phone lines; card sets for titles being cataloged at Rethymnon are now being computer-produced. Although there have been numerous discussions regarding extension of the on-line system to the UCR campus, a number of technical problems and bibliographic questions still need to be resolved.

In yet another development related to improved bibliographic control, King's College London and the University of Crete have embarked on a feasibility study, funded by the Commission of European Communities, regarding the cooperative retrospective conversion of library collections of European interest. If all goes as planned, the major university library collection of Greek-language materials in Europe outside of Greece, located at King's College, will be converted into machine-readable form according to international standards. The actual conversion will be carried out with the participation of library staff from UCR. Greek librarians will of course benefit, not only in honing their cataloging skills but also in gaining valuable experience in working in a major academic library. It is estimated that there is a 60-70 percent overlap between the King's College holdings and the modern Greek collections at the UCR library. Thus, successful completion of this project will enable the UCR library to use records from a substantial bibliographic database to catalog its own Greek-language materials. The availability of such a database should in fact be of great benefit to all Greek academic and research libraries and might well be the impetus for establishing national standards.

PUBLIC SERVICE

It was my observation that a strong commitment to public service exists at the University of Crete libraries. The facilities are open at times convenient to the users, and staff knowledgeable about the collections are generally available to provide simple reference assistance. In July of 1989, a new staff member, who is a recent graduate of the library training program in Thessaloniki, was hired to serve primarily as a reference librarian. In addition to providing direct service, she will also assume responsibility for building the reference collection and developing basic user guides and simple research bibliographies. The circulation and reserve-book systems that have been created are not cumbersome or restrictive, but rather encourage use of library materials. An automated circulation system is now being tested at Iraklion; if it is successful, it may be extended to the Rethymnon campus. Given available financial and staff resources, public service functions at the library are being remarkably well addressed.

MANAGEMENT

It is difficult to evaluate or comment on the Director's administrative style at the library because of the different approach to management in Greece when compared with that practiced in the

United States and Western Europe. A number of concepts taken for granted elsewhere are either unknown or difficult to implement (e.g., affirmative action, written job descriptions, standardized evaluations, formalized channels for input into the decision-making process, strategic planning, and operational efficiency). In the following section of this article, examination will be made of a number of external factors that influence the organizational environment, not only of Greek libraries but also of all sorts of other Greek administrative entities. The quality of supervision that I observed was humane and progressive. It was my sense that the staff took pride in its accomplishments and was stimulated and fulfilled by its work. Given the progress made by the library, it is obvious that Director Tzekakis understands the library's environment and is able to successfully negotiate for change.

EXTERNAL FACTORS INFLUENCING
GREEK ACADEMIC LIBRARIES

As the preceding narrative indicates, the accomplishments of the libraries at the University of Crete are substantive and the potential for continued growth and development are favorable. However, there are also continuing challenges that must be overcome. It is helpful to keep in mind that both the UCR and UCI libraries are functioning in an environment often shaped by external factors over which they have little if any control. As a result of both my own impressions and experiences (as well as many conversations with professional colleagues in Greece), it was possible for me to identify a number of factors influencing local library environment, not only in Crete but throughout Greece. These factors have been grouped together in the following general categories: national, higher education, and professional. Although some of the factors are not resolvable, simply understanding them, putting them into the appropriate perspective, and developing a strategy for coping can be helpful.

The National Level

1. *Political instability.* The country was in an "on hold" mode from 1988 through mid-1990 while a series of national elections

was held to determine if the government would be a conservative one or not. Given the impact and the leadership role of the national government in all phases of life in Greece, including cultural and educational endeavors, this was a time with little forward movement in problem resolution. Politics dominated the scene and consumed much of the creative energy of the country. This was understandable since the outcome of the elections would determine the government's position both philosophically and practically on a number of higher-education issues, including support for academic libraries. However, the resulting paralysis fostered a sense of frustration and stagnation among those waiting to get on with their work.

2. *Economic constraints.* Since all institutions of higher education, and indirectly most support for academic libraries, are funded by the national government, it is difficult in a time of high inflation and fiscal hardship to be optimistic about even adequate levels of support, let alone the possibility of governmental support for special library projects.

3. *Patronage.* Although not as excessive as in the past, there is still a patronage system in place in which personal relationships and extended family ties are frequently more important than ability and competence. Invocation of this patronage factor can do much to dampen the creativity and productivity of organizations and institutions.

4. *The ego factor.* The exaggerated sense of self that often characterizes the Greek persona can at times make cooperative efforts difficult. This quality came about, perhaps, as a result of the need to stand up against and survive 400 years of Ottoman rule. However, it can get in the way of creative group problem solving and can result in more rhetoric than action in the decision-making process. Even when apparent consensus is reached, a tendency still exists, by those holding the minority point of view, to delay or subvert implementation of that consensus.

5. *A strong hierarchical approach to management.* Determinations regarding working conditions, supervision, workflow, etc., when not specifically covered by union agreements, are frequently quite arbitrary in nature. There is little opportunity for substantive

consultation or participation in the decision-making process by those who may be most affected.

6. *Time concepts.* In Greece, the sense of time is more relaxed, with less of a feeling of urgency about meeting deadlines. Lags or delays in implementation of agreed-upon timelines are not considered as critical as they might be elsewhere.

Higher Education

1. *Teaching methodology at the university.* Although an increase is taking place in the number of classes taught at the university level by the system of "continuous assessment," which requires regular interaction between professor and student, with grades determined by classroom participation, submission of term papers and research projects–and periodic testing, the more common form of instruction–is still of the "traditional type." Faculty following the traditional method generally use the lecture mode and require that their students need only pass the final examination to complete the course. Preparation for the final consists of reading and usually memorizing the lecture notes and the content of books from a prescribed reading list. Examinations may be repeated until a passing mark is achieved. This traditional form of instruction requires little in the way of a general library facility–a departmental reading room or seminar with a small collection of the requisite titles usually suffices. Faculty who follow this traditional approach often feel that a strong, centralized library offering research support and broad collections is superfluous and, in fact, may be a threat to the departmental seminars. Conversely, faculty members using the continuous assessment approach tend to favor the establishment of centralized library collections. Since their students spend considerable time in the library doing research papers, it is more convenient to have research materials in a single location.

2. *Organizational structure in institutions of higher education.* Rectors (university presidents), vice-rectors, deans, and departmental chairs are elected by faculty for relatively short terms, sometimes annually. The elections are often highly politicized, and academic issues may not be the most important ones in the often heated election campaigns. These frequent changes of leadership mean that the management infrastructure is frequently in flux, trying to antici-

pate or respond to the changes at the top. The resultant instability makes long-term planning and priority setting difficult. With each change of rector, there is usually a change of emphasis. This constantly shifting organizational climate can lead to a disruptive and frustrating working climate in which permanent administrators can become increasingly inflexible in their relationships with subordinates. In an environment of crisis management, ad hoc decision making, rather than long-term and strategic planning, can become the rule.

3. *Poor management practices.* Questionable practices tend to crop up, especially in the areas of personnel and budget. For example, job descriptions and recruitment practices are casual at best. Written guidelines for evaluations and rewards for meritorious service are rare. Even the simplest of financial transactions can become a cumbersome and time-consuming process burdened by excessive checks and balances.

4. *Professional status of librarians.* Because the graduates of the library programs at the TEI lack a baccalaureate, librarianship still does not have much professional status in Greek universities. Teaching faculty and administrators often treat librarians, regardless of training and background, arrogantly and have little understanding of what the work of librarianship entails. Those librarians with an MLS degree from abroad or with advanced Greek university degrees have a better chance of commanding the respect and credibility requisite for any meaningful dialogue about the role of the academic library in the educational enterprise. It was my sense that a number of professors felt that anyone could do the job, since in their judgment it was basically clerical in nature. Many faculty members are unwilling to trust the professional decisions made by librarians or to permit librarians much latitude as participants in a team approach to academic planning issues. Illustrative of this concern is the strong, often aggressive, leadership stance that is assumed by the faculty library committee, which often functions as a shadow management team rather than as a consultative and/or advisory body.

The Practice of Librarianship in Greece

1. *Absence of a national bibliography.* Greece has neither a national bibliography nor a comprehensive listing of books published

in the country. Although the law requires that two copies of every book published in Greece be deposited in the National Library, the requirement is not rigorously enforced. Since publication of such a bibliography is a costly task with little promise of financial reward, the private sector is reluctant to take it on. At present, state funds are not available for the National Library to pursue the project. However, without such a publication, it is very difficult to define the scope of publishing in Greece or to begin the development of a comprehensive bibliographic database of materials published.

2. *Unresolved issues of bibliographic control.* The library community has not yet reached total agreement on how to deal with the following critical cataloging and classification issues:

a. Establishment of a standardized thesaurus of subject headings that can be used by all libraries in the country for both current and retrospective cataloging. It should be noted that the major international systems of subject headings are inadequate for the identification of works relating to the national heritage of Greece, especially in the areas of modern Greek language, literature, and history. Whatever system is selected as the basis for subject headings will have to be modified to ensure appropriate access to modern Greek materials. A related decision is where, how, and by whom the thesaurus will be maintained.

b. Determination of the language(s) to be used for subject access to library materials. If an augmented international scheme such as the Library of Congress Subject Headings is selected, it may be desirable, despite the immense effort required for translation, to have all subject headings in Greek. An alternative would be to use subject headings translated into Greek for all materials published in Greek and to use subject headings in English for all other materials, regardless of the language in which they are published. The issue is very sensitive and needs to be considered not only in the context of how to properly serve the research needs of the library user but also in the context of national concern about the degradation of the Greek language.

c. Expansion of the Dewey and Library of Congress classification schedules to provide for greater latitude in assigning call numbers for modern Greek materials.

d. Development of a comprehensive authority file of Greek

terms, place names, proper nouns, and personal names (which during the time of the Byzantine Empire and the Ottoman Empire had a multiplicity of forms).

e. Adoption of a standardized transliteration system for Greek and Latin characters to permit interfiling of materials written in the two alphabets and to facilitate the transmission of bibliographic data by computer.

f. Adoption by all Greek libraries of one of the three Machine Readable Cataloging (MARC) formats Library of Congress, United Kingdom, or Universal Machine Reading Cataloging (LCMARC, UKMARC, or UNIMARC) as the universal standard for formatting bibliographic information to facilitate computerized data exchange.

Despite repeated efforts to address these thorny issues, Greek librarians have been unable to come to terms with them. However, with the growth of academic libraries and the growing experimentation with computers for local bibliographic control, it is imperative that these questions be dealt with, if an imposed solution rather than a collective one is to be avoided.

3. *Fragmented leadership in the library community.* A strong professional library organization–united in its approach to library issues and able to articulate what the major needs are that face the profession–does not exist in Greece. Although a national library association exists, it has not been successful as an advocacy or lobbying group in winning support for library proposals, as has been the case with professional organizations in other countries. Nor has the National Library of Greece asserted itself as the vehicle for addressing nationwide library concerns. Similarly, the Ministry of Education, where library matters are addressed by the government, has failed to assume a long-term planning and coordinating role for libraries. Finally, university libraries, although aware of the need for the creation of a centralized body for discussion and action, have been unable to forge the appropriate coalition for action. Meetings are held, papers are read, and heated discussions occur, but nothing concrete comes of the rhetoric. The library community is fragmented, politicized, and primarily concerned with issues of protecting individual status and "turf." As yet, no group has emerged to take an appropriate leadership role.

PROSPECTS FOR THE FUTURE

The issues raised in the preceding section are not unique to the situation in Crete, but rather are concerns that must be dealt with by all academic libraries in Greece. Although the list may seem overwhelming, the situation is far from bleak. Problem definition is the first step in developing an agenda for change, and it is my sense that there is an increasing awareness and concern about library issues among my professional colleagues in Greece. Some of the factors identified are not related to matters that can be resolved, but placed in proper perspective, their harmfulness is diminished.

However, those issues that relate directly to librarianship can be addressed. In the past, bickering and questions of turf and individual status have thwarted cooperative efforts, but this situation may be changing. The King's College retrospective conversion project, the increasingly strong professional relationship being developed by the libraries at the University of Thessaloniki and Kent State University, the high quality of the library training program at the Thessaloniki TEI, and the continued work in the field of library automation at both the Universities of Crete and Thessaloniki are all signs of great vitality. As Greece becomes a full participant in the European Economic Community, opportunities for additional international cooperative programs will increase. These activities are not only important individually but also collectively because they create a climate for progress and growth as well as fostering an enthusiasm among Greek academic and research librarians for tackling the big issues still facing them.

From the time of the establishment of the University of Crete in 1974, Director Tzekakis and his colleagues, both in Rethymnon and Iraklion, have played a vital role in promoting the concept of academic libraries that are responsive to the needs of students and faculty alike. Given limited financial and staff resources and a myriad of other problems, the level of accomplishment is remarkable. Always open to advice and counsel, Tzekakis has encouraged visits to Rethymnon by foreign colleagues and asked for their suggestions regarding the local library situation. Input that he feels is practical and feasible is often incorporated into the operation of the two libraries at his institution. He is a man of unflagging enthusiasm and dedication. That the libraries at the University of Crete serve as a role model for other newly developing university libraries in Greece is testimony to the imagination, insight, and productivity of his library. Much has been accomplished. Much remains to be done. However, I am most optimistic of the outcome.

The Library of Aristotle University of Thessaloniki: Organization, Operation, and Perspectives

Nicolaos Alexandrou
Dimitrios Dimitriou

The Central Library of Aristotle University was established in 1927, two years after the founding of the University. The Library's main goal is to serve and inform about 1500 faculty members and 50,000 students in the ten different Schools of the University. These schools are:

- School of Theology
- School of Philosophy and Foreign Languages
- School of Sciences
- School of Law and Economics
- School of Health Sciences
- School of Agriculture
- School of Technology
- School of Education
- School of Fine Arts
- School of Physical Education and Athletics

The Central Library is housed in a building of four floors. It contains a 1,000-desk reading room for students and a reading room for faculty members, graduate students, and researchers. These reading rooms are open daily, and on weekends, from 8:00 a.m. to 8:30 p.m. The Library has an auditorium, with 120 seats, designed for lectures, workshops, and other similar activities. Equipment for reading and photocopying microfilm and microfiche is available, and there is a room for exhibitions.

The Central Library holds about two million volumes and sub-

This article was translated by Athena Salaba.

scribes to approximately 3,500 periodicals, covering all fields of knowledge. The collection grows by approximately 25,000 purchased volumes and 3,000 donated volumes each year. This makes it the largest academic library in Greece. There are twenty employees in the Central Library, as well as four high school teachers and ten practicum students each semester from the School of Library Science of the Technological Educational Institution of Thessaloniki. The Library is directed by a special administrative officer, and is supervised by a Faculty Committee. The Committee's members are selected from the University's Senate every three years. The Library's Director serves as a liaison to the Committee. Online Computer Library Center (OCLC)-Europe was installed at the Central Library in 1989. The University community is served by several CD-ROMs. Soon, additional databases will be available as well.

The University's library system includes a network of twenty-five branch libraries that are associated with various academic departments. These libraries will be connected with the Central Library by a computer network being installed by the University; thus, they will have access to an on-line union catalog that will provide information on all books and periodicals in the Library system. Plans are being made to establish a computer connection between the Central Library of Aristotle University and the Library of the University of Crete and, eventually, with the Kent State University Libraries.

The Central Library cooperates with the Libraries of Kent State University, and several staff members from our Library have pursued graduate studies in the School of Library Science at Kent State University or have gained practical experience in the libraries there. Also, faculty members from Kent State University's libraries have visited the Central Library at Aristotle University to collaborate with our staff in developing the Central Library's services and arrangements. The Central Library's staff attends continuing education lectures and workshops on librarianship.

In addition to providing current services, the Central Library is working on a project to organize its collection of rare books and to publish a catalog of this collection. Plans are also being made to give lectures on the use of CD-ROMs, OCLC, and on-line reference service, and there is a long range goal of establishing a School of Library Science in the Aristotle University of Thessaloniki.

The Library of the Department of English Language and Literature at the Aristotle University of Thessaloniki, Greece

Alex Noel-Tod

INTRODUCTION

In the spring of 1989, I was invited by the British Council to visit the Department of English at Aristotle University to review the present holdings of English and American literature in their library and to advise on its development. Initially, the request was for advice on the development of the collection of primary texts on English and American literature, but it was recognized that any such expansion of the present collection could only go hand in hand with the general development of the stock, staffing, administration, and arrangement of the Library. Extra bookstock has little value to the reader if it cannot be cataloged, classified, shelved in an understandable and accessible manner, and made available in a suitable environment.

The department's request to the British Council asked for "someone able to come in and locate the gaps, first of all, and secondly, to suggest more efficient methods of operation." This was a fairly tall order for me to fulfill in under six working days, with access to the library limited to much shorter hours than is common in UK academic libraries. Much of the time I could gain access to the bookstock had to be spent in carrying out a detailed check of particular holdings in order to indicate the degree of underprovision in the stock. This assessment constitutes the most specific part of my report. In addition, however, I spent time determining the size of the constituent parts of the collection. Beyond that, I attempted to gauge what needed to be done in the way of general library orga-

129

nization and administration, staff training, etc., but I am very conscious that my recommendations in those areas are based on the most hurried impressions and on incomplete observations and conversations with library staff and faculty. I was also able to make a brief tour of all the other departmental libraries in the New Philosophy Building, which gave me an indication of the general state of library provision and organization. In addition, I was taken around the University Library.

I was fortunate in that a visiting librarian from Kent State University Library, Mr. Dean H. Keller, who was at that time resident in the University Library, was extremely generous in sharing with me the findings of his longer experience on campus. He also gave me copies of the reports of two of his Kent State University colleagues who had worked in the English Department Library during the academic years 1985-86 and 1986-87. Those documents are cited within this report (Birk 1986; Murphy 1987).

Despite strike-delayed travel, altered schedules, strikes on campus, and other changes to plans, I completed as much as I did thanks largely to the hospitality and cooperation of the faculty and library staff. Dr. Ruth Parkin-Gounela, Professor Gina Politi, and Dr. Giorgos Kaloyeras were most helpful both in arranging my stay and informing me on library and faculty matters. Fotini Stavrou and Eleni Dota in the library bore with remarkable good humor my dogged attempts to get answers to involved, technical questions while they attempted to deal with more pressing matters of library services. That I was able to learn so much about the stock and operation of the library in so brief a time was due in large measure to the help they gave me. This report does not deal with the provision of library material for language teaching and linguistics, though there are references to the stock size, etc.

LAYOUT OF THE LIBRARY
AND SIZE OF THE COLLECTION

The library has been formed by the partitioning of a larger area that includes faculty teaching and administration offices. The library consists of a bookstock area on two levels that are connected by a small spiral staircase. The stacks on the lower level are given over to the cataloged monograph stock, with sections for a collection of reference works and a collection of multiple copies of course texts and photocopies. The upper level is given over to the journal collection and to a backlog of unprocessed/unsorted material. The lower level also accommodates the card catalog, a desk for the librarian on duty, and a desk for the electric typewriter for catalog card production, etc. There is also some working space upstairs.

Conditions in the stack areas are very cramped, which is aggravated by the fact that access and exit is by a single door in the partition between the stacks and reading room. A visiting librarian wrote in 1987: "The general work area of the library is quite inadequate (more than 4 people in there at one time makes it difficult to move)" (Murphy 1987). That situation still prevails.

The reading room is in an area between windows and the lower stack area. There are twelve large reading tables, seating either six or eight, giving a maximum seating capacity of 92 places. I was told that at busy times of the year most seats would be taken. I made head counts at various times during my visit and found that attendance fluctuated between 17 and 38 readers, inclining toward the lower figure. The back wall of the reading room has an unused bookstack, comprising nine bays of five shelves per bay. There was no other library furniture in the reading room, except for a display rack with a selection of publishers' catalogs and related ephemera. Lighting for the reading room was from fluorescent strip lighting on the ceiling.

While not unfriendly, the library environment for readers was, all in all, bleak and noisy. The partitioning offered little by way of noise reduction, and the noise from the neighboring faculty offices "jumped" over the open space of the upper level of bookstack and carried quite clearly into the reading room–not just conversation but music from a radio, the clatter of typewriters, photocopiers, etc. It was impossible for the library staff to be other than disruptive of any "library quiet," with all their equipment positioned in a single area close to the reading room.

Stack Capacity

I estimated that the total stack capacity was approximately 20,000 volumes; this would include commissioning the unused shelves in the reading room and instituting a separate sequence for oversize books. Doing so would allow the majority of the book-stacks to be shelved out on a standard "five shelves to a bay" pattern in order to maximize the use of present capacity. At present, the space for the monograph collection on the lower level is nearly exhausted, and it will soon be necessary to continue the sequence on to the upper level.

Monograph Collection Size

Subject	LC Classmark(s)	Number of Titles
Linguistics and language	P and PE	880
General and comparative literary theory and criticism (including film, general drama, etc.)	PN	550
English Literature	PR	1650
American Literature	PS	1050
Other literatures and languages	PA-PD, PG-PQ, PT	250
Non-literary subjects (including general encyclopedias and other general reference works)	A-NX, Q-Z	730
Shelved Bookstock		5110

Backlog	
Cataloged material awaiting creation of catalog cards, processing of books, etc.	800
Material (shelved downstairs) requiring cataloging	350
Material selected by Alex Noel-Tod as being of next priority from remaining unsorted material (upstairs)	300
Shelved Bookstock and Backlog	6560

The total of 6,560 different *titles* should be supplemented by the significant number of extra copies of some works. Thus, the total *volume* estimated for the bookstock would be 7,000-7,500 volumes. In addition to the above categories of material, there is a residue of

the ex-British Council, ex-University Library, and previous departmental library collection that amounts to about 1,500-2,000 volumes (not titles). Much of this is not worth adding to stock, since it
is obsolescent, irrelevant, in poor condition, etc., and will need to be
disposed of as the shelf space is needed for the expansion of the
processed collection.

Recommendations:

1. Consider removing the partition between bookstacks and reading room to allow for easier access, etc.
2. Rather than have the security provided by the work area at the
   end of the lower stacks, move the duty librarian's desk out into
   the reading room area to provide both the inquiry service and
   security over access/exit to the combined stack/reading area
   (this pattern has been established in other libraries in the same
   building).
3. Use the empty bookstack in the reading room for the general
   reference section of the Library, possibly a display of current
   journal issues or the like.
4. Move the card catalog out into the reading room area (much of
   the present congestion arises from the fact that readers want-
   ing access to the stacks are blocked by readers consulting the
   catalog, and both groups tangle with those going to the librarian's desk to make loans, inquiries, etc.)
5. In the space created at the end of the stack area (by removing
   the reference section, the card catalog and the duty librarian's
   desk, etc.), create a work counter behind which could be
   shelved the short-loan collection, multiple copies of course
   texts, etc. This could be the work area for catalog card production, book processing, etc. This area should be arranged to
   provide an equivalent surveillance over the library's entrance/
   exit as that offered by the other desk in the reading area and
   would also allow for times when only one librarian is on duty.
6. In the stack sequence for bookstock, create a separate sequence for the minority of books from all classes over a certain
   height (except possibly those shelved in the general reference
   section). This would allow for maximum use of a standard
   shelving sequence. The "oversize books" location could be
   indicated on the relevant catalog entries.

7. Consider ways of reducing the intrusion of noise from the faculty offices (at present, there is no partitioning of the upper stacks on that side).
8. Consider lessening the direct sunlight element from the reading room windows (this will be necessary if the reading room area is to hold any part of the bookstock–see Recommendation 3 above).

PRIMARY AND SECONDARY TEXTS: ENGLISH AND AMERICAN LITERATURE

To gauge the present provision in certain areas of the collection, a selection of British and American authors was chosen from the bibliographies included in Volumes 9 and 10 of the *New Pelican Guide to English Literature* (NPGEL) (Volume 9: *American Literature* [1988]; Volume 10: *A Guide for Readers* [covering Volumes 1-8] [1984].) A survey was also made of certain sections of the bibliographies of historical/critical works on English and American literature, including the bibliographies of critical studies on two major authors, W. B. Yeats and T. S. Eliot.

Obviously, the NPGEL bibliographies can be faulted in various particulars, but they do have the merit of making a sustained attempt to give attention to most periods and major authors. I noticed that various volumes of the NPGEL were being used in the teaching of the department, and they were featured among the course texts distributed to students. It seemed reasonable to expect the library to stock NPGEL items as part of its basic provision. In the case of some twentieth century authors, it was necessary to draw from lists outside the NPGEL volumes; some author bibliographies were selected from two standard reference works, *Contemporary Poets* and *Contemporary Novelists* (indicated in the lists by "C"). In the bibliographies of secondary texts, a check was also made against the literature collections in the University of East Anglia Library (UEA). See the following lists for the survey results.

British Authors: Pre 1900	Primary text holdings as percentage of author's published canon	
WYATT, Sir Thomas	1503-1542	0
SPENSER, Edmund	1552-1599	25
CHAPMAN, George	1559-1634	0
MARVELL, Andrew	1621-1678	85*
COWPER, William	1731-1800	45
FIELDING, Henry	1707-1754	50*
POPE, Alexander	1688-1744	50
SMART, Christopher	1722-1771	0
CLARE, John	1793-1864	15*
CLOUGH, Arthur Hugh	1819-1861	0
GASKELL, Elizabeth	1810-1865	85
DICKENS, Charles	1812-1870	70
STEVENSON, Robert L.	1850-1894	30

British Authors: Early 20th Century	Primary text holdings as percentage of author's published canon	
AUDEN, W. H.	1907-1973	30*
BENNETT, Arnold	1867-1931	40*
COMPTON-BURNETT, I.	1884-1969	0
DOUGLAS, Keith	1920-1944	75
ELIOT, T. S.	1888-1965	50
HARDY, Thomas	1840-1928	70
LAWRENCE, D. H.	1885-1930	60
OWEN, Wilfred	1893-1918	0
SASSOON, Siegfried	1886-1967	10
WAUGH, Evelyn	1903-1966	45
YEATS, W. B.	1865-1939	50

British Authors: Later 20th Century	Primary text holdings as percentage of author's published canon	
AMIS, Kingsley	1922-	20
BAINBRIDGE, Beryl	1934-	40
BROOKE-ROSE, C.	1926-	0 C
BUNTING, Basil	1900-1985	0 C
DAVIE, Donald	1922-	0*
DUNN, Douglas	1942-	0 C
DURRELL, Lawrence	1912-1990	60
FRY, Christopher	1907-	50 C
GASCOYNE, David	1916-	10*
GORDIMER, Nadine	1923-	10
GUNN, Thom	1929-	0
HEATH-STUBBS, John	1918-	0 C
HUGHES, Ted	1930-	15

JENNINGS, Elizabeth	1926-	0 C
JOHNSON, Jennifer	1930-	0 C
JONES, David	1895-1974	0
LARKIN, Philip	1922-1985	20*
LEVI, Peter	1931-	10 C
McEWAN, Ian	1948-	20 C
McGUCKIAN, Medbh	1950-	0 C
NARAYAN, R. K.	1906-	0
PRINCE, F. T.	1912-	0 C
RIDLER, Anne	1912-	0 C
SCANNELL, Vernon	1922-	0 C
SILKEN, Jon	1930-	10 C
THOMAS, R. S.	1913-	0 C
TOMLINSON, Charles	1927-	0
TREVOR, William	1928-	0
WILSON, A. N.	1950-	0 C

American Authors: All Periods	Primary text holdings as percentage of author's published canon	
ANDERSON, Maxwell	1880-1959	15
BALDWIN, James	1924-1987	50*
BARTH, John	1930-	45*
BERRYMAN, John	1914-1972	0
BRAUTIGAN, Richard	1935-	50
CALDWELL, Erskine	1903-1987	15
CARVER, Raymond	1938-	0 C
CREELEY, Robert	1926-	15
DICKEY, James	1923-	10
DIDION, Joan	1934-	0
DONLEAVY, J. P.	1926-	0
FRENEAU, Philip	1752-1832	0
GADDIS, William	1922-	0 C
GLASGOW, Ellen	1874-1945	20
HUGHES, Langston	1902-1967	15
JEWETT, Sarah Orne	1849-1909	10*
KEROUAC, Jack	1922-1969	10
LARDNER, Ring	1885-1933	0
LONDON, Jack	1876-1916	5
LOWELL, Robert	1917-1977	10
MALAMUD, Bernard	1914-1986	60
NORRIS, Frank	1870-1902	15
PERCY, Walker	1916-1990	0
PORTER, Katherine A.	1890-1980	15
ROTH, Philip	1933-	45 C
SIMON, Neil	1927-	0
SONTAG, Susan	1933-	40 C
THURBER, James	1894-1961	0

WARREN, Robert Penn	1905-1989	30 C
WELTY, Eudora	1909-	70
WILLIAMS, William C.	1883-1963	20
WOLFE, Thom	1900-1938	15 C

*Some material in uncataloged backlog

Primary and Secondary Texts: Conclusions

From my limited survey, it was apparent not only that the provision of primary texts of major authors was extremely uneven but also that the average level of representation was noticeably low (around 35 percent success rate). While it would be unrealistic to expect a 100 percent level of coverage in primary texts, it should be possible to expect even a newly formed academic library to attain a success rate of 60 percent and over. All the authors I surveyed are currently in print in a variety of editions; while it may not be possible to get every desired scholarly edition, a good variety of academic editions are usually available for major authors. Pursuing research into a particular author may be beyond the present scope of the library, but it should be possible for faculty or students to expect the library to contain individual texts of an author's major works.

It was apparent that much selection of secondary texts was on the basis of individual faculty interest, and this led to significant differences in success rates. A current interest in teaching black/ethnic literature shows in the American table, as does a particular interest in medieval English literature. But the overall success rate was alarmingly low; even if I had counted the titles held in those areas not listed in the NPGEL, the average success rate would not have been above 30 percent.

The present annual funding of approximately 3 million drachma would be reasonable if its primary task was to maintain an already well-stocked collection. However, the collection is nowhere near that state; since purchases cost more than for an equivalent institution in the U.K. or U.S.A., the present level of annual funding will never allow for the necessary "quantum leap" in collection development. Recommendations:

1. The department should seek capital funding of at least 10 million drachma, available over a period no longer than three

years. This would be a special grant *in addition* to the continuance of the annual funding of 3 million drachma. The capital grant would be for the purchase of primary texts in literature, language, and linguistics. The purchases would be made on a systematic basis from defined bibliographies and lists, not just a "spend" against an accumulation of individual faculty recommendations. It might be necessary for the department to engage an external consultant to assist in this policy.

2. With regard to required items no longer in print, a desiderata file should be maintained and cooperation sought with UK or US dealers and/or libraries willing to act as agents to supply such desiderata.

JOURNALS

The library's journal holdings were slight, with most titles being represented by short runs often containing incomplete years. There was also a very small number of current subscriptions.

Current Subscriptions

For the whole field of literature and linguistics, there were fourteen current subscriptions. That number was determined by the professorial strength of the department; current subscriptions were paid for (and received) by the University Library. This small number was supplemented by the purchase of certain serials (e.g., the *MLA Bibliography*) out of the book allocation on a year-by-year basis. Because the subscriptions were tied to a funding formula that both severely limited the choice and made it subject to individual faculty choice, there was evidence of cancellations and switches in selection, with the result that many journals were represented by only two or three years of subscription. As a result, they were almost useless in terms of future exploitation.

Back Runs

Very few of the one hundred or so journal titles represented by back runs were held completely or even for substantial periods.

Some of the more sustained runs were there as a result of the donation of ex-library material by the British Council (e.g., the reprint of *Scrutiny*, or a nearly complete run of *Poetry Review* from 1912 to 1982). Most titles were held in runs of no more than three to five years. The library has no journal holdings in microform, and there appeared to be no such holdings for literature and linguistics.

Condition, Arrangement, and Identification

The journals were all shelved on the upper floor and arranged in a single alphabetical sequence by title. Only one or two of the donated back runs were bound; the rest were placed directly on the shelves in unbound parts.

A typed list exists that indicates titles and holdings, as well as those titles having current subscriptions. This is not a complete list of serials in the library, since certain items have been treated as part of the book collection (e.g., *American Literary Scholarship*). There is no public index for journals (e.g., wall- or table-mounted strip-index or section of the card catalogue), and there is no display area for current parts received.

Use of the collection seemed slight and individual–reflecting its profile of changing faculty interests rather than any basic provision for the curriculum. I surmised that faculty usage of journals must be largely dependent on: (a) the fortunate chance of the library's holdings matching an individual's need, (b) personal subscription, or (c) the use of study leave, etc., in other European or American academic libraries to gather the necessary journal material for teaching and research.

Journal articles that were required reading for courses seemed to be provided either by their reproduction in anthologies or made available to students as photocopies. Conclusions:

1. The journal coverage is inadequate by any criteria. This was also a conclusion reached in both Kent State University reports. In 1986, Nancy Birk wrote that the *"MLA Bibliography* is the only indexing tool [available] and unfortunately the library has only a few of the journals it indexes. . . ." In 1987, Patricia Murphy stated that "[for] a graduate program . . . [i]t will be necessary to spend a considerable amount of money

just to develop the journal collection and to build journal back-runs. . . . There is a definite lack of current journal subscriptions. If the Department intends to require research of its faculty and students it will be necessary to increase the journal subscriptions. . . . [B]efore this [graduate] program is started there needs to be a massive upgrading of the collection and the journals (both current and retrospective)."

Even though journal selection/coverage has to be a fairly subjective exercise in choosing from among the enormous number of titles covering literature and linguistics, a collection of fourteen titles is far too small. By way of a benchmark test, the faculty might like to consider the fairly modest list proposed by McPheron (1981) as a suitable basis for a small college library serving the curriculum for a BA in English; after excluding McPheron's categories of "Author journals" and "Little magazines," the count is still 54 titles. Recommendations:

1. Funding should be sought for a larger number of current subscriptions. This funding should be arranged so as to ensure some degree of continuity in subscriptions.
2. There should be a "core" of current subscriptions that attempt a basic overall provision for literature and linguistics, both generalist academic journals and review journals; these titles should not be considered candidates for substitution when titles required for individual research interests, etc., are being chosen.
3. There should be provision on campus of microform holdings of backruns of major literary journals. Since viewing equipment is available in the University Library, it might be best to collect such titles there.
4. A more accessible public list of holdings should be devised, and, as part of the rearrangement of the reading room, suitable furniture provided to mount a display of current issues received.
5. The present collection of backruns should be reviewed to assess the practical value of keeping short, incomplete runs of unbound issues in the collection and to monitor the relevancy of some of the titles held. Shelf space is too limited to allow the indefinite retention of "dead" or irrelevant material.
6. It is probably not worth considering binding any of the back-

runs, but material that is to be kept should be shelved in open pamphlet boxes.

BOOK ORDERING

The system of standard recommendation forms and two-part order slips seemed to work well enough. The main problems with the system were: (a) the efficiency of the supplier and the cost of supply and (b) the lack of any commitment accounting. My analysis of the order file showed that:

- On order from orders placed in
  June or September 1988   400 titles (approximate)
- With supplier awaiting arrangement
  of payment   200 titles (approximate)
- Unfulfilled orders prior to June/
  September 1988   500 titles (approximate)

During the current year, the receipt of orders was:

- Items arrived from orders placed 1987-88   167 titles
- Items arrived from orders placed 1988-89   545 titles
- Orders received 1988-89 to April   712 titles

The order "failure rate" appeared to be 15-20 percent; that is, the number of times which, in any year, orders would never be fulfilled. This is a high rate for such a small volume of generally straightforward items. The supplier did report back on progress with certain items. The evidence of the order file suggested that many items failed to arrive, probably because of weaknesses in the supplier's procurement system with U.K./U.S. distributors/publishers. It was also apparent from the evidence of recent invoices that there was a premium of 10-12 percent over and above the U.K.-/U.S.-recommended retail price of most items. Exchange control difficulties and unfavorable exchange rates probably contributed to the premium. There was no discount available on the purchase of U.K./U.S. books, and it seemed that it was difficult to arrange direct supply through U.K./U.S. library suppliers. Exchange control, etc., also made it difficult to purchase secondhand material through U.K./ U.S. specialist outlets.

Commitment Accounting

The present ordering system is largely driven by the collection of faculty recommendations at one or two points in the year and by the sending off of large orders in anticipation of one or more "lump sums" becoming available from the annual faculty grant. The main concern is to ensure that any sums allocated are spent up within the same year, otherwise they can be subject to "callback" by the university; the evidence of a surplus could prejudice future allocations. Such a system makes it difficult to budget, or work, a system of rolling targets that allows annual carry-over of balances. There appeared to be no breakdown of actual/committed expenditure between subject areas (e.g., English literature, American literature, Linguistics, etc.). Recommendations:

1. That orders be monitored on a regular basis, both to check on efficiency of supply and on the average cost of items.
2. That at least a notational system of budgeting and commitment accounting be instituted (even if the "lump sum" financing has to remain), so that there is some idea of different subject expenditure as well as the general progress of expenditure.
3. Faculty should investigate liaison with U.K./U.S. general or specialist library suppliers, possibly with the cooperation and advice of a U.K. academic library, which in turn might be able to act on an agency basis.

CLASSIFICATION

The bookstock is arranged by the Library of Congress (LC) Classification Scheme. The classification is determined from the LC catalogue record. The classmark is taken exactly as given, with no local variations. The advantage of this policy is that it can be administered by library staff without detailed knowledge of LC schedules, cuttering methods, etc., and it creates a shelf arrangement that follows one order, even if that order is not always appropriate. It also means that using the classmark as given in the catalogue record ensures a match between the information transcribed from the LC catalog record and the shelf label. This may sound like an obvious benefit, but in all the other libraries I saw on campus there was no single, unified classification scheme in existence; nor was there necessarily a correlation between catalogue records and classmarks. I was told that students thought one of the benefits of this library was the fact that the information in the catalogue matched the shelf order–and also that the shelf order manifested itself as an understandable system!

The disadvantages of following, without variation, LC classification as given in the LC catalogue records is:

- The classification exhibits the changes made to LC over the years without any local attempt at standardization. Thus, changes in the details of the LC scheme are displayed according to when the original LC catalogue entry was made. On the whole, this is a minor fault, though it will be magnified as the collection grows and there is a greater mixture of old and newly published material.
- The classification follows certain practices in LC that contradict the logic of an academic collection. The most serious of these is the recent LC practice of putting all works of fiction in Class PZ, instead of putting them with their authors in PR or PS. Already, there are works of major modern literary figures divorced from their appropriate place in PR or PS and put in this rag-bag class. To prevent this requires some reclassification by library staff, which might not be a problem when an appropriate PR or PS classmark exists. It is more difficult when there is no precedent for them to follow.
- Another disadvantage in absolute adherence to LC information regarding shelf order is that there is a splitting up of reference works. While there is a "reference section" at the beginning of the book sequence that in effect pulls out certain items from the main book sequence, there are also a large number of major reference works shelved right at the end of the main book sequence in Class Z. Many of the latter should be in the

"reference section"; these should also have their appropriate subject classmark rather than the LC choice of Z. This requires some practical knowledge and manipulation of the LC schedules to achieve.

There appeared to be no public chart to explain the classification scheme to readers, nor did the staff possess copies of the classification schedules published by the Library of Congress. I did pick up a single-sided sheet that explained very briefly the layout and logic of an LC "call number" (e.g., "How to locate books by call number"). Recommendations:

1. The Library should purchase certain volumes of the LC schedules (at least those for classes P-PN, PR, and PS). This would support any local need to amend received LC information.
2. Library staff should receive further instruction in the application of the LC classification scheme, so that they are able to use the schedules to allocate classmarks when an alternative to the "received" LC Catalog information is required.
3. Class PZ should not be used; suitable alternative locations in the author sequence for PR, PS, etc., should be found. Those books already in Class PZ should be relocated.
4. Items in Class Z should be reviewed to determine which should be relocated in the reference section (possibly with a different classmark).
5. A poster-size chart should be produced to show the main classes in the LC classification scheme; a more detailed handout on classes P-PN and PR and PS might also be appropriate. The poster and the handout could be displayed/available in the reading room.

CATALOGUING

There is a card catalogue with Author/Title/Subject divisions. The catalogue exactly replicates the entries for those items in the Library of Congress Catalog, including all necessary added entries. Cataloguing is done by transcribing in manuscript the record found in the LC Catalog, then typing this onto cards using an electric typewriter with a memory/repeat facility. Enough copies of the entry are produced to provide for the over-typing of all the added entries. The obvious disadvantage and inefficiency of this system is the enormous amount of time and effort required to create entries for a single monograph. For example:

* The monograph must be matched with the entry in the LC Catalog (unless adequate Cataloging-in-Publication (CIP) data is printed inside the book). This means working with the LC Catalog housed in the University Library, largely a job that can only be done in vacations.
* The LC Catalog entry is copied in entirety in manuscript (including collation, notes, ISBN, etc.).
* The manuscript slip is then typed to recreate, in effect, the printed LC entry.
* Sufficient copies of this whole entry are then created by the typewriter to give sufficient copies for all the added entries indicated on the LC entry.
* An extra copy is created to act as the shelflist copy; this is the only copy that gives the item's accession number and records the number of copies in stock.

The main advantage of this system is that, as with the classification, it allows the library staff to create a fully fledged catalogue without the need to create catalogue records themselves. And, indeed, the result is a splendidly detailed catalogue with full-dress descriptive cataloguing, but lacking the necessary infrastructure of cross-references, reconciliation of subject-heading changes, etc. In terms of the information required by the local user, this seems to be a case of overkill. It may be a standard suitable for a major library's catalogue, but it is extravagant for a departmental library. The labor-intensive aspect is emphasized by the present backlog/throughput of the system.

In April 1989, the backlog consisted of 700-800 titles with manuscript LC Catalog entries awaiting the production of typed cards, processing of books, etc. (many of these books were given their ms. entries by the Kent State University librarian in 1986-87). The throughput is figured over a working year of about 40 weeks, at 60 titles transcribed per week. Though this may equal 2400 entries transcribed per year, it results in a smaller total in terms of completed and filed catalogue entries and processed books. The staff attempts to balance throughput between new purchases and material in the backlog; nevertheless, it is evident that it will become increasingly difficult to cope with both new purchases and the backlog, particularly if the faculty is successful in obtaining extra funds for purchases.

Catalogue Furniture

The card catalogue comprises 54 drawers:

* Author: 7
* Title: 7
* Subject: 10
* Shelflist: 6
* Empty: 24

The catalogue needs respacing. An estimate of the effective unused balance is no more than 20 drawers. This means that a catalogued bookstock of approximately 5000 volumes has created a card catalogue (excluding the shelflist) of some 30 catalogue drawers. Each catalogued item generates an average of 5.5 cards. Recommendations:

1. That the present cataloguing system be reviewed to (a) make it less labor-intensive and (b) to increase the rate of throughput. (Faculty might seek advice from the University Library where a computerized cataloguing system, Online Computer Library Center (OCLC) Europe, is being installed; faculty might also utilize a "look-alike" of that system that could be mounted on a stand-alone microcomputer and so be used to catalogue departmental libraries.)
2. Library staff should be trained to have some cataloguing ability.
3. The card catalogue should be respaced, and the unit should be moved out into the reading room area, thus making it more accessible and also increasing the staff work area (see the recommendations under "Layout").

STOCK CIRCULATION
AND LOAN PERIODS/PROCEDURES

Present loan periods for students are 9:00 a.m. to 1:00 p.m.
(Monday, Wednesday, and Friday) and 9:00 a.m. to 1:00 p.m. and
3:00 p.m. to 7:00 p.m. (Tuesday and Thursday). An item can be
borrowed on deposit of a student's registration card. Though the
bookstock has been processed with pocketed tickets to allow the
operation of a "Browne" issue system, these are not used for student loans. The brevity of the loan (and the total volume of loans)
make it uneconomical to maintain an issue file. Instead, brief details
of the borrowed item are noted by the staff and attached to the
deposited registration card.

Student loans seem very short (though many other departmental
libraries allow no loans to students, and there is no open access to
the stock in the University Library), and this is a source of com-
plaint. Much of the present student demand is for the multiple
copies of course texts, including photocopies, or for other "directed
reading" in the reserve collection. There was little evidence of
loans from the "non-directed" part of the bookstock.

Staff loans are, in effect, of indefinite length. An annual recall
request is sent out by the library, but there is no sanction for not
heeding it. Analysis showed that 1200 items were presently on loan
to staff. The majority had been borrowed during the period October
1988 to April 1989, but there was a significant number of loans still
outstanding from 1986, 1987, and the first half of 1988. For staff
loans, the book tickets are kept as an issue file, and staff also sign
the items out on their page in a staff loans register. Recommendations:

1. Student loans should be divided between (a) short loans for
   course material in demand (photocopies, bookstock placed on
   reserve by faculty, and multiple copies–all this material should
   be kept in the short loan collection specified in my recommendations under "Layout") and (b) longer loans (a week?),
   which should be allowed during termtime for material in the
   general bookstock.
2. Staff loans should be subject to at least a recall each term, and

faculty should consider some sanction to ensure that material is returned at the annual recall.
3. A proper loan file should be maintained at least for loans made on a weekly or termly basis, and a system of recalls, reservations, etc., should be implemented.

STAFF ORGANIZATION AND TRAINING

It might seem curious to leave this matter until the end of the report, since it is the keystone in virtually all other matters discussed. The successful implementation of many of the recommendations in this report depends entirely on the capabilities of the library staff.

I do not intend to go into much detail on the present staffing of the Library; my visit was too short to get a proper perspective, and the period was disrupted by industrial action on campus. Nevertheless, I would like to record that, viewing other libraries on campus and realizing the progress made since the first Kent State University report in 1986-87, I am certain that the department is fortunate in, and well served by, its library staff.

The day-to-day running of the library-including all library procedures such as issues, enquiries, cataloguing, creating orders, etc.–is carried out by two library assistants. They work a 35-hour week: yet in order to cover the varying range of opening hours on different days, they work for periods that only coincide for 18 hours per week. Though their supervision is a responsibility held by a faculty member, they depend largely on self-administration to organize and apportion library duties. The main disadvantages in the present situation (noted both from my own observation and from discussing the matter with the staff in post and with the responsible faculty member, Dr. Parkin-Gounela) are:

1. The training they have received from the library school at Thessaloniki (at the TEI) is based largely on the public library sphere, and this certainly does not draw on a tradition of experienced teachers from other library sectors, nor can it offer fieldwork in established academic libraries. This makes it difficult for the staff to create an organization of which they have little knowledge or previous experience.

2. The supervision by faculty cannot remedy this situation since the latter are, of course, not conversant with the technicalities of the relevant "good practice" and its implementation.
3. The faculty's training lacks practical experience with appropriate methods of cataloguing and classification. The previous visits of the two Kent State University librarians have given them some knowledge of Library of Congress schemes, but there is a pressing need for the experience of working in an established academic collection where these schemes are in operation.
4. The present staffing levels are inadequate, given the methods of work, to maintain anything more than a pretty modest throughput of work in developing the collection. The small amount of communal work time, the demands of serving readers, etc., makes it difficult for them to establish efficient and effective work patterns (certainly in termtime). Furthermore, this inadequacy will be emphasized if the department is successful in obtaining capital funding to increase the collection, and if it implements other recommendations in this report.
5. The lack of experienced professional library staff, and the low level of professional cooperation throughout the campus, makes it difficult for the staff of one departmental library to seek advice and guidance on general matters of library organization. (Indeed, there is a certain mandarin quality in the departmental libraries; on one visit, I was prohibited from asking innocuous questions of professional interest about their computerized database until I had the permission of the head of the department!).

Recommendations:

1. The department should consider ways of improving the professional experience of the library staff, not only to equip them with the necessary skills and expertise but also to provide them with the knowledge and confidence to implement developments in the library service. One way this could be achieved would be through a three-month (minimum) secondment to a U.K./U.S. library, where training and work experience could be offered that was most pertinent to the development and

organization of the Department's library. In addition to the practical experience of working in a U.K./U.S. library, the secondment should offer a program of visits to other libraries, etc. If such a secondment was to a U.K. library, it is probable that the arrangement of such a secondment would benefit from the involvement of the British Council.

2. The department should consider staffing levels for the library, bearing in mind the staffing/workload implications of other recommendations in this report.

3. The department should see if it can obtain local professional advice on library matters from other library staff. Inquiries to other departmental libraries might reveal areas of common "good practice" and suggest training initiatives.

BIBLIOGRAPHY

Birk, Nancy. 1986. "The English Department Library at the University of Thessaloniki: A Report on the Realities and the Ideals." Unpublished report.

McPheron, William, ed. 1987. *English and American Literature: Sources and Strategies for Collection Development.* Chicago: American Library Association.

Murphy, Patricia. 1987. "English Department Library, Aristotle University of Thessaloniki, 1986-1987." Unpublished report.

New Pelican Guide to English Literature. Vol. 10: A Guide for Readers. 1984. Harmondsworth, England: Penguin Books.

New Pelican Guide to English Literature. Vol. 9: American Literature. 1988. Harmondsworth, England: Penguin Books.

A User Survey
of the English Department Library
at Aristotle University,
Thessaloniki, Greece

Martha Kyrillidou

INTRODUCTION

Greek academic libraries are different from their American counterparts, and one of the differences lies in the fact that the Greek libraries are not necessarily independent entities within a university but instead are independent entities within academic departments. These are mostly and primarily defined by the department to which they belong. Therefore, the focus of this user survey is a specific departmental library, the Library of the English Department at Aristotle University, in Thessaloniki, Greece.

The largest university in Greece is Aristotle University of Thessaloniki, with approximately 55,000 to 60,000 students. The University, which was founded in 1925, consists of 12 schools, composed of 36 departments.[1] There is a central library and 98 officially registered libraries. This figure changes, since libraries sometimes merge or new ones are created. It is probable, though, that the officially registered libraries may not represent an equal number of physical locations. Once the departments receive the books they have ordered, there is no control as to where and how the books are stored, organized, and disseminated. Responsibility for these matters lies with faculty within the departments.

The Central Library receives and catalogs the books for the entire academic community, and then sends them to the departments. There is an effort being made to systematize the classification of materials in the smaller libraries.[2] Bibliographic control over the collections of the libraries in the Aristotle University is exercised through the existence of two main catalogs found in the Central Library. One, the old catalog, which covers the period up until 1982, does not follow Anglo-American Cataloging Rules, second edition (AACR2). The classification system used is an old, obsolete German system based on accession numbers. The second catalog represents the books the university acquired after 1982. Cataloging follows AACR2 rules, and the classification system is the Library of Congress system.

In departmental libraries, there is no uniformity of standards of library operation or policies. Each departmental library is financially dependent on the specific department to which it belongs, and a department may have more than one department library. To provide a frame of reference, the following figure provides a comparison between Kent State University and Aristotle University. The data approximate the real figures.[3] (See Figure 1.)

THE ENGLISH DEPARTMENT

The English Department is one of seven departments in the School of Philosophy. The other departments are Education-

FIGURE 1. Comparison Chart Between Aristotle University and Kent State University

	Aristotle	KSU
faculty	2,282	1,118
students	56,000	22,753
faculty/student ratio	1:24	1:20
volumes	300,000 Central	
	1,600,000 (Total)	1,646,327
library staff	26 (Central)	184

Psychology-Philosophy, Philology, History-Archaeology, French, Italian, and German. Although there are only seven departments in the School of Philosophy, there is not an equal number of departmental libraries, since some of the departments have three and four libraries. The English Department has one library. The books are classified according to the Library of Congress system of classification, and there are two full-time librarians (technical college graduates) working there. The library is considered to be one of the best departmental libraries on campus, because a well-kept card catalog is maintained, and the books are shelved according to the classification system. The library underwent major organizational changes in 1985-1987, when two American visiting librarians worked there for nine months each.

The collection is kept in closed stacks, but students are allowed to enter the stacks area as long as they leave their belongings outside. The collection is used only for reference (i.e., there is no official circulating system in operation). Students are allowed to use the books within a study area adjacent to the closed stacks. Despite the fact that books are not lent outside the study hall or for more than one day, students appear to use the library and the adjacent study hall quite heavily. The main asset of this library seems to be access to the information needed, whereas in other departmental libraries that is often a luxury. The library operates an official circulation system for the faculty members, who are allowed to borrow as many volumes as they want for as long as they want.

The library of the English Department has been constantly evolving and developing, and that is one of the major reasons that it is the focus of this study. In 1989, a visiting librarian from Britain made a report on the development of the collection, identifying major gaps in the collection and submitting recommendations.[4] This current study focuses on the clientele of the library, exploring user characteristics and attitudes toward the library.

This study is the first user survey of a Greek academic library, and it is important for the following reasons. First, the question of exploring and describing the community of the library of the English Department is of interest in itself, since this library stands as a model within the academic community. It is one of the best-organized departments on campus in terms of bibliographic control, and it provides a not-often-met advantage in a Greek academic departmental library–user access to the collection. It should be noted that there are a number of reasons for the existence of that advantage: (a) almost all of the collection is composed of English books, which makes the cataloging process efficient and cost-effective; (b) for two years, two American visiting librarians worked there and organized the collection; and (c) all the faculty members have been exposed to Anglo-American information retrieval systems.

The English Department has repeatedly been the focus of attention of visiting library consultants. Carnovsky, in his recommendations for academic library education in Greece, points out that a library science department could be founded and operated with the same status as the English Department.[5] Palmer, fifteen years later, in his recommendations for a graduate library school, suggests that the proposed school should be attached to the English Department at either the University of Thessaloniki or the University of Athens.[6]

Additionally, graduates of the English Department are more likely to choose library science as a profession, in contrast to university graduates from other departments. The reason can be the positive exposure these students have to the library of the department, as well as to the British Council Library and the American Center Library in Thessaloniki. Some graduates of the English Department in fact choose to receive a library science degree in the United States. Last, the present investigator has a close knowledge of this department, both as a past student and as a user of the library.

An additional contribution of this study relates to the methodological issues encountered in the development of a user survey in a Greek academic library. User surveys are not standardized, not even in the case of American libraries. The variables of interest in a user survey have traditionally been library-specific, and generalizations are avoided. This study explores the variables of interest in a Greek departmental library and defines and measures these variables.

PURPOSE OF THE STUDY

The purpose of this study is to explore:

1. The characteristics of the users of the English Department library at Aristotle

2. The patterns of library use
3. The attitudes of both the students and faculty toward the library

The characteristics of potential and actual users are investigated. In particular, in a quest for user characteristics, data on variables such as sex, GPA, academic class, place of origin, inclination toward the specific field of study, and future goals are collected to see how they are related to use of the library.

What are the reasons people have for using this academic library? An investigation of the possible reasons for patrons' use of the library includes an analysis of whether people use the library to study their own materials, use library materials, and/or complete specific assignments. The frequency of particular library uses is also examined.

How well is the library perceived to fulfill its role? What are the users' expectations of the library? The participants of the survey are asked to express their attitudes and level of satisfaction with existing library conditions. The present study provides one measure of assessing existing library conditions through users' perceptions. The knowledge of the present is the only stable basis upon which future planning can be built. As Geoffrey Ford says:

the general objective of research on users is to further understanding of the processes of information transfer. The research may be expected to lead to improvement of information transfer systems and to have implications for the organization of communication, the distribution of resources and the relationship between systems.[7]

This study tested a tool that can be used elsewhere to collect information about Greek academic libraries. Such information is not generally available. The information collected in this instance should be useful to the library of the English Department as well as to persons concerned with the fortunes of Greek academic libraries and librarianship.

LIMITATIONS

This study has certain limitations. It does not examine the administration and operation of the library of the English Department. It focuses on the users of the library, their characteristics, and attitudes toward the library. For the purposes of this study, the following requirements are presumed to apply: the departmental library should occupy a designated area in which the books are stored; books should be shelved according to the Library of Congress classification system; access to the book collection should be available through a card or on-line catalog that can provide at least three kinds of access points (author, title, and subject); both faculty and students should have access to the collection; and a designated person, preferably a librarian, should be responsible for administering the library's programs.

Activities considered as library use in this study include use of the library as a study hall, borrowing library materials, checking the card catalog, using reserved books, browsing through the collection, and asking librarian's assistance in using the library. The specific frequency of library use examined in this study is weekly. Nonusers means respondents who did not enter the library during the week of the study. This is one of the major limitations of the study, and it should be kept in mind when examining the results. Nonusers are actually irregular and infrequent users, rather than people who have never used the library.

For the library of the English Department, a weekly indication of library use is judged to be adequate for a pilot study because of the proximity of the library to the department itself. Most departmental libraries in Greece are located within its own department, and so weekly use of the library can be regarded as defining regular library users. Such usage also judged to be adequate for potential cross-departmental comparison.

There are also methodological limitations arising from the focus of this study on library users. The main one, inherent in all such surveys, is that the validity of the results depends on the sincere response of the population members surveyed and their ability to recall past events accurately and precisely. Another inherent problem in statistical analysis of surveys is the "limitation of generalization."[8] The results are generalized to the specific sample examined (i.e., the sample drawn from the English Department). Conclusions drawn about this group can be "verified by restudy in a population of greater importance."[9] Moreover, the fact that the observations will concern subjects of "a particular educational background . . . who happen to be attending a particular institution of higher education at that moment in time"[10] should be kept in mind. It is open to speculation to what extent generalizations about other academic libraries in the Aristotle University can be made, because of the highly decentralized character of the system.

The sample is self-selected, since participation in the survey was voluntary and no means of enforcement was exercised. Finally, there are theoretical limitations and handicaps in utilizing the user approach. These include: (1) arbitrary distinctions among actual users, potential users, and nonusers and (2) limited perspectives based on subjects' perceptions that do not necessarily constitute reality.

METHOD

For purposes of this study, the survey method was adopted. The primary tools developed and used were: (1) a questionnaire for faculty and (2) a questionnaire for students. The students and the faculty of the English Department are the major users of the library of the English Department. Theoretically, a user of the library of the English Department can be any member of the academic community, but in practice this library is almost exclusively used by students and faculty of the English Department. Therefore, the population in this study consists of all the students and all of the faculty members of the English Department.

Currently, the Department of English has approximately 1,600 students enrolled. This figure, however, does not represent the active population (i.e., the population that regularly attends classes), since it includes people who have dropped out of their studies. The active population of the department is approximately 1,200 students. Of this number, approximately 60 percent attend classes. The number of faculty members surveyed are forty, including visiting professors and graduate assistants.

The questionnaire for the students was distributed and collected in their classes at the beginning or end of the class period. The actual visits to the classes occurred during one week, which was the last week of classes during the spring semester of 1989. No follow-up procedures were established for the students.

The questionnaire for the faculty was mailed, and follow-up procedures were completed within four weeks from the initial distribution of the questionnaires. A 60 percent response rate was considered sufficient for the purposes of this study. (Copies of student and faculty questionnaires are found in Appendixes 1 and 2.)

The development of the survey was based on user survey activity in American libraries. Most of the variables included are found in American library user surveys.[11] There are, however, variables included that are uniquely appropriate to Greek academic libraries. Inclusion of these variables was arbitrary to a large extent and based on the researcher's judgment. There is no previous research on Greek academic libraries that validates these decisions.

Measuring library use is problematic, and conclusions drawn must be library-specific. For purposes of this study, two basic measures were developed. One is activity-related and the second has to do with frequency of library use. An arbitrary decision had to be made concerning what constitutes an adequate indicator of frequent usage in a Greek academic library. The period of observation for this study is, as stated above, weekly library use.

DATA NEEDED

The questionnaires request the following information from users:

1. Demographic and personal data.
2. Reasons for use or not of departmental library and frequency of use of this and other libraries.
3. Data concerning the quality of the library as perceived by the users and of suggestions concerning improvement in library hours, instruction, facilities, and services.

For the students, the following data are requested: sex, cumulative GPA, academic class, their hometown population, their inclination towards a specific field of study, and their future objectives.

For the faculty, the following data are requested: sex, highest academic degree, length of service in the department, and faculty rank. These data are necessary for the grouping of the respondents into different categories for further analysis.

DESCRIPTION OF THE SAMPLE

The period for the collection of data lasted one week. Seven hundred and fifty questionnaires were distributed to the students and forty-one to the faculty members. Four hundred and fifty-six (60%) of the questionnaires were returned by the students and twenty-five (60%) were returned by the faculty. A summary of the demographic characteristics of the student and faculty respondents is presented in Tables 1 and 2, respectively.

Student Sample

The respondents are heavily weighted toward females. This reflects the student population makeup, which has a strikingly unequal distribution between the two sexes. Traditionally, the School of Philosophy attracts more women than men, especially in the foreign-language departments.

Grade point average (GPA) in the Greek universities has a scale of zero to ten, with five as the minimum requirement to pass a course. Only 8% of the respondents have a GPA between 8.5 and 10, which roughly approximates what would be considered an A in an American university. More than half of the respondents (54%) in the sample have a GPA between 7 and 8.49; 38% average between 5.5 and 6.99.

As far as size of academic class is concerned, there are more third-year (33%) and first-year (31%) students than second-year (18%) and fourth-year (18%) students. This anomaly probably is accounted for by a flaw in sampling procedure. During the semester the data were gathered, there were obligatory courses for first- and third-year students but not for second- or fourth-year students. Because the questionnaires were distributed and collected in the classrooms, data collection was simple but imperfect.

TABLE 1. Summary of Characteristics and Demographics Related to the Students

		n	%
SEX	Male	37	(8%)
	Female	415	(92%)
	Total	452	(100%)
GPA	8.50-10.00:	34	(8%)
	7.00- 8.49:	234	(54%)
	5.50- 6.99:	162	(38%)
	Below 5.49:	2	(−)
	Total	432	(100%)
Academic Class	Fourth year	82	(18%)
	Third year	148	(33%)
	Second year	83	(18%)
	First Year	142	(31%)
	Total	455	(100%)

Was the English Department your first choice for an academic career?

	n	%
Yes	377	(83%)
No	79	(17%)
Total	456	(100%)

If you could choose again, would the English Department be your first choice?

	n	%
Yes	350	(78%)
No	98	(22%)
Total	448	(100%)

What is the population of the city or town or village in which you grew up?

	n	%
500,000 or more:	200	(44%)
100,000 to 499,999:	41	(9%)
50,000 to 99,999:	64	(14%)
12,000 to 49,999:	76	(17%)
less than 12,000:	74	(16%)
Total	432	(100%)

Are you planning to go to work immediately after graduation?		
Yes	330	(73%)
No	119	(27%)
Total	449	(100%)

Are you planning to continue your studies through a second Bachelor's, Master's, or Ph.D. later on in your career?		
Yes	238	(54%)
No	204	(46%)
Total	442	(100%)

Eighty-three percent of the respondents indicated that the English Department was their first choice for an academic career; when they were asked whether it would have been their first choice if they could choose again, 78% said that it would be.

The majority of the respondents (44%) came from cities with a population of more than 500,000 (i.e., either from Thessaloniki or Athens). Interestingly, with the exception of the two largest cities, a pattern can be observed in the distribution of the students and the size of the town or village from which they came: the number of students increases as the size of town or village decreases. A possible explanation is that there are more small towns in Greece than medium-sized ones. It is possible, too, that there is motivation on the part of the students to leave the small places for study in large cities–and the smaller the area, the more motivated they seem to be.

The overwhelming majority of the respondents plan to go to work immediately after graduation (73%). However, more than half of them (54%) plan to continue their education as well.

Faculty Sample

The majority of the faculty respondents were women (16, as opposed to 9 men). One of the respondents had a bachelor's degree, thirteen had master's degrees, and eleven had PhDs. Eight assistants

TABLE 2. Summary of Characteristics and Demographics Related to Faculty

	n	%
Sex:		
Male	9	(36%)
Female	16	(64%)
Total	25	(100%)
Highest Academic Degree:		
Bachelor	1	(4%)
Master	13	(52%)
Ph.D.	11	(44%)
Total	25	(100%)
Faculty Rank:		
Graduate (EMY)	4	(16%)
Assistants toward a Ph.D.	4	(16%)
EEP teachers	5	(20%)
Lecturer	1	(4%)
Assistant Professor	4	(16%)
Associate Professor	4	(16%)
Professor	3	(12%)
Total	25	(100%)
Length of service in the English Department:		
1-2 years	9	(38%)
3-5 years	2	(8%)
6-9 years	6	(25%)
10+ years	8	(29%)
Total	25	(100%)

(both graduate assistants and instructors), five EEP (*Eidiko Ekpe-deutiko Prosopiko* [i.e., Special Education Personnel]), one lecturer, four assistant professors, four associate professors, and three professors responded to the questionnaire.

Most of the respondents had worked in the English Department for only a very short time; however, some had worked there for more than five years. Thirty-eight percent had worked there for one or two years, and more than fifty percent of the respondents for more than five years. Only two respondents (8%) had been employed there for three to five years.

REASONS FOR LIBRARY USE

Table 3 reports reasons for library use. The majority of the students (66%) use the library to borrow library materials. A large proportion (44%) of the student body uses reserved books. The third reason for student use of the library is for studying their own materials (28%). Very few students use the card catalog; fewer visit the library to get information from the librarian; only two percent browse through the collection, probably because the stacks are designated as a restricted access area.

Students use the library almost twice as many times to use library materials as to study their own materials (Table 4). Therefore, the library does not serve exclusively as a study hall, which has been a popular assumption in the department. Students enter the library primarily to use library materials 52 percent of the time; 28 percent

TABLE 3. Reasons for the Use of the Library Last Time the Respondent Entered the Library

Reason	Students		Faculty		Total	
	n	%	n	%	n	%
Study own materials	127	(28%)	4	(16%)	131	(18%)
Borrow library materials	295	(65%)	21	(84%)	316	(44%)
Check the card catalog	7	(2%)	10	(40%)	17	(2%)
Use reserved books	199	(44%)	2	(8%)	201	(28%)
Browse through	11	(2%)	5	(20%)	16	(2%)
Ask something of librarian	17	(4%)	5	(20%)	22	(3%)

TABLE 4. Reasons for and Frequency of the Use of the Library by Students on Weekly Basis

	none		1 to 3		4 to 9		Total	
	n	%	n	%	n	%	n	%
Study own materials	325	(72%)	112	(25%)	13	(3%)	449	(100%)
Study library materials	215	(48%)	217	(48%)	17	(4%)	449	(100%)
Complete assignment	337	(75%)	103	(24%)	5	(1%)	445	(100%)

to use their own materials; and 24 percent to complete a specific class assignment.

The majority of the faculty (84%) visits the library to borrow library materials (Table 3). A large proportion of them (40%) enter the library to check the card catalog. Twenty percent of the reasons for entering the library involves browsing in the collection or asking something from the librarian. Only 16 percent of the faculty uses the library to study their own materials, probably because their offices are close by.

The overwhelming majority of the faculty prefers to use materials at home (64%) (Table 5). Thirty-two percent, however, prefers their office to study. Only four percent use the library as a study area.

FREQUENCY OF USE

Students are, of course, frequent users of the library (Table 6). In the present sample, it was found that 37 percent of the students had not used the departmental library in the week before the survey; 55 percent used it from one to three times; and 8 percent of the students used it from four to nine times. As for the faculty data, 16 percent did not use it at all; 17 percent used it one to three times; and 16 percent used it four to nine times.

TABLE 5. Preferred Faculty Location for Studying

Location	n	%
Office	8	(32%)
Library	1	(4%)
Home	16	(64%)
Total	25	(100%)

TABLE 6. Frequency of the Use of the Library on Weekly Basis

	none		1 to 3		4 to 9		Total	
	n	%	n	%	n	%	n	%
Students	165	(37%)	250	(55%)	35	(8%)	450	(100%)
Faculty	4	(16%)	17	(68%)	4	(16%)	25	(100%)

NONUSE OF THE LIBRARY

Students who did not enter the library were asked to indicate their reasons (Table 7). Ninety students (20%) checked as a reason that they had no need to use it. Forty students (9%) claimed that the library was not open when they wanted to go to it; twenty-nine students (6%) said that they did not have time; eleven (2%) indicated that they found the books they needed elsewhere; and eight (2%) said that the library did not have the materials they wanted. Faculty indicated that the biggest reason for non-use of the library was that the books they needed were found elsewhere.

When asked whether they were using other libraries, 219 students (48%) and twenty-one faculty members (84%) indicated that they were. Those who answered yes to this question were asked to indicate which libraries they use (Table 8). Most said they use the British Council Library. The proximity of this library to the campus could explain this.

TABLE 7. Reasons for Nonuse of the Library for Faculty and Students

	Students		Faculty	
	n	%	n	%
I didn't have time	29	(6%)	1	(4%)
I didn't need it	90	(20%)	3	(12%)
It was not open when I wanted to go	40	(9%)	1	(4%)
It did not have the materials I needed	8	(2%)	1	(4%)
I found the books I needed elsewhere	11	(2%)	25	(100%)

TABLE 8. Other Libraries Used by Faculty and Students

	Students		Faculty	
	n	%	n	%
Central Library	50	(11%)	4	(16%)
British Council Library	154	(34%)	10	(40%)
American Center Library	93	(21%)	4	(16%)
Public Library	15	(3%)	2	(8%)
Other	15	(3%)	12	(48%)

USER AND NONUSER RESPONSES

For purposes of this study, students who indicated no use of the library during the previous week were considered infrequent users or "nonusers." Students who indicated that they used the library once or more during the previous week were considered to be frequent users or, as they are labeled here, simply, "users." Table 9 presents the demographic characteristics of users and nonusers. A careful examination of the results reported in this table shows that more regular users of the library have higher grade point averages, are less likely to go to work immediately after graduation, but tend instead to continue their education.

TABLE 9. Summary of User/Nonuser Characteristics for Students

		Nonuser		User	
		n	%	n	%
SEX	Male	13	(8%)	24	(8%)
	Female	150	(92%)	261	(92%)
	Total	163	(100%)	285	(100%)
GPA	8.50-10.00:	9	(6%)	25	(9%)
	7.00- 8.49:	78	(49%)	153	(57%)
	5.50- 6.99:	70	(44%)	91	(34%)
	below 5.59:	1	(1%)	1	(–)
	Total	158	(100%)	270	(100%)
Academic Class	Fourth Year	27	(17%)	54	(19%)
	Third Year	54	(33%)	93	(32%)
	Second Year	25	(15%)	56	(20%)
	First Year	58	(35%)	84	(29%)
	Total	164	(100%)	287	(100%)
Was the English Department your first choice for an academic career?					
	Yes	142	(86%)	233	(81%)
	No	23	(14%)	54	(19%)
	Total	165	(100%)	287	(100%)
If you could choose again, would the English Department be your first choice?					
	Yes	121	(74%)	255	(82%)
	No	43	(26%)	55	(18%)
	Total	164	(100%)	310	(100%)

TABLE 9 (continued)

	Nonuser		User	
	n	%	n	%
What is the population of the city or town or village in which you grew up?				
500,000 or more:	73	(45%)	125	(44%)
100,000 to 499,999:	14	(8%)	27	(9%)
50,000 to 99,999:	27	(16%)	36	(12%)
12,000 to 49,999:	24	(15%)	51	(18%)
less than 12,000:	26	(16%)	48	(17%)
Total	164	(100%)	287	(100%)
Are you planning to go to work immediately after graduation?				
Yes	129	(79%)	198	(70%)
No	34	(21%)	85	(30%)
Total	163	(100%)	283	(100%)
Are you planning to continue your studies through a second Bachelor's, Master's, or Ph.D. later on in your career?				
Yes	77	(47%)	161	(58%)
No	86	(53%)	115	(42%)
Total	163	(100%)	276	(100%)

Table 9 shows that, proportionally, library users have higher GPAs. Proportionally, more nonusers (86.1%) chose the English Department as the department in which they would like to pursue an academic career than did library users (81.2%). However, if they could choose again, the English Department would be the first choice for fewer library nonusers (73.8%), whereas it would be a first choice for more library users (82.2%). It appears that library users are more sure than are nonusers as to what they expect of an academic career.

Students who come from the two largest cities, Thessaloniki and Athens, are almost equally split between users (43.6%) and nonusers (44.5%). More nonusers (25%) come from medium-sized towns (users are 22.9%). Fewer nonusers (20.5%) come from towns with a population of under 49,999 inhabitants than do users (34.5%). Table 10 shows that the reasons both frequent users and infrequent users enter the library are comparable. The first reason is to borrow library materials; the second is to use reserve books; and the third is to study one's own materials. Table 11 shows that more frequent users tend to use more other libraries than do nonusers.

ATTITUDES TOWARD THE LIBRARY

The third part of the questionnaire measures student and faculty attitudes toward the library. The attitude used was a four-point Likert scale, with "1" indicating strongly disagree, "2" indicating disagree, "3" indicating agree, and "4" indicating strongly agree. The last choice is not applicable, and these responses are treated as

TABLE 10. Reasons for the Use of the Library for Users and Nonusers

	Nonusers	Users	Total
Study own materials	35	91	126
Borrow library materials	107	185	212
Check the card catalog	–	7	7
Use reserved books	68	130	198
Browse through	4	7	11
Ask something from librarian	7	–	7

TABLE 11. Use/Nonuse of Other Libraries by Users and Nonusers of the Library of the English Department

	Nonusers		Users	
	n	%	n	%
Yes	70	(42.4%)	149	(51.9%)
No	95	(57.6%)	138	(48.1%)

missing data. The higher the score, the more positive the attitude toward the library. A few items that indicate negative attitudes are reverse-coded. Table 12 presents the survey findings.

Table 13 presents descriptive statistics for users and nonusers on an eight-point satisfaction scale. Items have been recoded so that the higher the score, the greater the satisfaction. Users have consistently higher satisfaction levels than do nonusers.

Lastly, more users than nonusers favor the introduction of a formal course in library instruction (Table 14). The changes that both frequent users and nonusers would like to see in the library are similar (Table 15). The change needed most concerns library hours. The second most desired change is the establishment of an official circulation system. The third is improvement in the library environment. The last is the establishment of open stacks. Only eight respondents (four users and four nonusers) indicated that no changes are necessary.

The results of attitudes toward the library are presented in three tables. Table 16 interprets faculty responses, item means, and standard deviations. Because the faculty sample is very small, the results are merely suggested. Item means and standard deviations for students are presented in Table 17. Student attitudes are more readily interpretable because of the larger number of responses from students.

Six items in both faculty (items 24, 28, 31, 18, 27, and 29) and student (items 28, 32, 35, 22, 31, and 33) questionnaires are identical. These serve the purpose of exploring what the role of the library is perceived to be. The first three items examine the role of the library in relation to its function (research, teaching, or both), and the second triad explores the role of the library in relation to its clientele (faculty, students, or both). The respondents had to indicate the degree of agreement or disagreement with each of the six items.

In an effort to determine whether the respondents distinguished between the library's primary and secondary functions (and between primary and secondary clientele), those respondents that consistently differentiated among the three items examining the function of the library and among the three items examining the clientele of the library were extracted. Two new variables (one

TABLE 12. User/Nonuser Attitudes Toward the Library

		Nonuser		User	
		Mean	SD	Mean	SD
17)	My professors and lecturers require that I use the library for specific assignments.	2.87	.66	2.97	.66
18)	The library provides services that are important to me as an individual.	2.66	.75	2.97	.69
19)	The items I want from the library are always available.	1.82	.71	1.93	.73
20)	The books are easy to locate.	2.34	.76	2.44	.76
21)	The library is noisy.	2.54	.85	2.57	.88
22)	The library of the English Department serves primarily faculty.	2.66	.74	2.67	.67
23)	The library hours are convenient.	1.91	.79	1.73	.75
24)	The quality of my departmental library's collection is very good.	2.36	.75	2.46	.69
25)	The size of my departmental library's collection adequately meets my needs.	2.29	.76	2.44	.77
26)	The library is a pleasant place to visit.	2.29	.76	2.50	.76
27)	The use of the library affects the students' final grade.	2.60	.83	2.84	.81
28)	The library of the English Department is important primarily for teaching purposes.	2.40	.66	2.35	.70
29)	Use of the library is important for the academic success of the students.	2.82	.70	3.08	.73

TABLE 12 (Continued)

		Nonuser		User	
		Mean	SD	Mean	SD
30)	My professor and lecturers recommend the use of the library.	3.19	.51	3.15	.62
31)	The library of the English Department serves primarily students.	2.62	.70	2.64	.72
32)	The library of the English Department is important for both teaching and research.	2.85	.72	3.01	.66
33)	The library of the English Department serves both faculty and students equally.	2.53	.74	2.63	.75
34)	The library is too crowded.	2.75	.73	2.90	.67
35)	The library of the English Department is important primarily for research purposes.	2.62	.77	2.45	.72
36)	The library is clean and neat.	2.68	.66	2.82	.65
37)	The library doesn't have enough places to sit.	2.63	.77	2.75	.70

related to the function and the other to the clientele of the library) were computed according to the way subjects responded to these items. For example, for the variable related to the function of the library, a subject is considered able to differentiate if the subject agrees or strongly agrees that the library is important primarily for research purposes (item 31 in the faculty questionnaire and item 35 in the student questionnaire) and, at the same time, indicates disagreement or strong disagreement with items suggesting that the library's purpose is for teaching (item 24 in the faculty questionnaire and item 28 in the student questionnaire) or both teaching and research (item 28 in the faculty questionnaire and item 32 in the student questionnaire). The new variable describing the clientele of

TABLE 13. User and Nonuser Satisfaction

		Nonuser		User	
		Mean	SD	Mean	SD
38)	Library service	4.68	1.86	4.98	1.90
39)	Library materials for research	4.55	1.76	4.59	1.76
40)	Library materials for teaching	4.63	1.57	4.71	1.65
41)	Library materials for students	4.69	1.73	5.17	1.76
42)	Book collection	4.60	1.91	4.94	1.72
43)	Reserve materials	4.58	1.78	4.90	2.40
44)	Staff help	4.67	2.23	4.90	2.40
45)	Physical environment	4.49	2.01	4.45	1.98

TABLE 14. User/Nonuser Opinion on Library Instruction

	Nonusers		Users	
	n	%	n	%
Yes	115	(84.6%)	230	(92.4%)
No	21	(15.4%)	19	(7.6%)

the library is defined in a similar way. The three levels of the clientele of the library are faculty, students, or both. The data for subjects who did not respond differently are treated as missing data.

Interestingly enough, only 188 students (41%) and ten faculty (40%) respondents differentiated among the different levels. Hence, there was no agreement concerning the role of the library as one of research, of teaching, or of both. The rest of the respondents do not distinguish between primary and secondary functions of the library. In regard to the clientele levels of the library, only 158 students (34%) and fourteen faculty (56%) distinguished between primary

TABLE 15. User and Nonuser Responses on Changes that Would Increase Satisfaction with the Library

	Nonuser	User
No changes necessary	4	4
A New circulation system, with library cards	57	84
Open stacks, i.e., books stored in open shelves	40	45
Changes in the environment (e.g., lighting, heating, furniture, etc.)	48	73
Changes in the library hours	61	160
Other	7	15

and secondary clientele. The rest of the respondents made no distinction.

Of respondents who differentiated among the levels of the function of the library, the majority of the students (135) and faculty (8) indicated that the library is important primarily for research purposes. Moreover, the majority of the students (66) indicated that the library serves primarily faculty. Five faculty respondents make the same distinction as the students, and six indicate that the library serves the faculty and students equally (Table 18).

The question that arises is why so few respondents differentiated consistently among these levels. Two possible explanations may be given. One relates to the way the survey was constructed and the other to the role of the library. The respondents were presented with a Likert scale; they were not forced to make a choice, and they did not. The second explanation has to do with the role of the library. Libraries have no clear-cut priorities, or as librarians say, "There is always something for everybody in every library." Therefore, the respondents cannot differentiate.

The following analysis of user attitude examines student data only because of the limited number of responses from the faculty. The question to be explored is whether frequent or infrequent use (labeled as "nonuse") of the library scored differently on the attitude scales. Four respondents strongly agreed with the statement, three agreed, two disagreed and one strongly disagreed. Table 19

TABLE 16. Faculty Attitudes Toward the Library

		Mean	SD
13)	I require that the students use the library for specific assignments.	3.60	.58
14)	It provides services that are important to me as an individual.	3.37	.92
15)	The items I want from the library are always available.	1.90	.92
16)	The books are easy to locate.	3.04	.62
17)	The library is noisy.	2.91	.71
18)	The library of the English Department serves primarily students.	2.26	.75
19)	The library hours are convenient.	2.20	.76
20)	The quality of my departmental library's collection is very good.	2.17	.71
21)	The size of my departmental library's collection adequately meets my needs.	1.70	.90
22)	The library is a pleasant place to visit.	2.47	.79
23)	Use of the library affects the students' final grade.	3.04	.76
24)	The library of the English Department is important primarily for teaching purposes.	2.47	.73
25)	Use of the library is important for the academic success of the students.	3.50	.51
26)	I recommend the use of the library.	3.76	.43
27)	The library of the English Department serves primarily faculty.	2.31	.83
28)	The library of the English Department is important for both teaching and research.	3.13	.75
29)	The library of the English Department serves both faculty and students equally.	2.30	.82

TABLE 16 (continued)

		Mean	SD
30)	The library is too crowded.	3.04	.49
31)	The library of the English Department is important primarily for research purposes.	1.95	.89
32)	The library is clean and neat.	2.45	.58
33)	The library doesn't have enough places to sit.	2.52	.77

TABLE 17. Student Attitudes Toward the Library

		Mean	SD
17)	My professors and lecturers require that I use the library for specific assignments.	2.93	.66
18)	The library provides services that are important to me as an individual.	2.86	.73
19)	The items I want from the library are always available.	1.89	.72
20)	The books are easy to locate.	2.40	.76
21)	The library is noisy.	2.56	.87
22)	The library of the English Department serves primarily faculty.	2.67	.69
23)	The library hours are convenient.	1.80	.76
24)	The quality of my departmental library's collection is very good.	2.43	.71
25)	The size of my departmental library's collection adequately meets my needs.	2.38	.76
26)	The library is a pleasant place to visit.	2.37	.69
27)	Use of the library affects the students' final grade.	1.80	.76

TABLE 17

		Mean	SD
28)	The library of the English Department is important for teaching purposes.	2.37	.69
29)	Use of the library is important for the academic success of the students.	3.01	.80
30)	My professors and lecturers recommend the use of the library.	3.17	.58
31)	The library of the English Department serves primarily students.	2.63	.71
32)	The library of the English Department is important for both teaching and research.	2.95	.68
33)	The library of the English Department serves both faculty and students equally.	2.60	.75
34)	The library is too crowded.	2.85	.70
35)	The library of the English Department is important primarily for research purposes.	2.52	.74
36)	The library is clean and neat.	2.77	.66
37)	The library doesn't have enough places to sit.	2.71	.73

reports the mean scores for users and nonusers. In most of the items, the users scored consistently higher than the nonusers. Not unexpectedly, users have a more positive attitude toward the library.

SATISFACTION

The questionnaire also included a satisfaction index made up of eight items that indicated different services and operations of the library. Subjects were asked to indicate their satisfaction with each one of these services and operations on a scale of one to eight (Table 20). The items have been coded, so that a high score indicates high satisfaction.

TABLE 18. Role of the Library–Differential Responses

Function of the library	Students	Faculty
The library of the English Department is important primarily for research purposes	135	8
The library of the English Department is important primarily for teaching purposes	27	2
The library of the English Department is important for both teaching and research	26	–
Total	188	10
Clientele of the library		
The library of the English Department serves primarily students	41	3
The library of the English Department serves primarily faculty	66	5
The library of the English Department serves both faculty and students equally	51	6
Total	158	14

The mean satisfaction score is higher for users, lower for infrequent users, and lower still for nonusers. No visits to the library during the last week was an indicator of nonuse; one to three visits to the library was an indicator of use; and more than four visits was an indicator of frequent use of the library. Satisfaction level increased with increased use of the library.

CHANGES

The majority of the students (77%) and faculty (76%) would like to see a formal course on how to use the library offered to the students (Table 21). Only 9% of the students and 10% of the faculty responded negatively.

The change chosen as the one that would most increase subjects' satisfaction with the library is related to library hours (Table 22).

TABLE 19. T-tests on Attitudes for Users and Nonusers for Students Only

		Number of Cases	Mean	SD
ITEM 17	Nonuser	156	2.87	.66
	User	260	2.97	.66
ITEM 18	Nonuser	151	2.66	.75
	User	266	2.97	.69
ITEM 19	Nonuser	156	1.82	.71
	User	280	1.93	.73
ITEM 20	Nonuser	156	2.34	.76
	User	280	2.44	.76
ITEM 21	Nonuser	162	2.54	.85
	User	286	2.57	.88
ITEM 22	Nonuser	137	2.66	.74
	User	256	2.67	.67
ITEM 23	Nonuser	158	1.91	.79
	User	280	1.73	.75
ITEM 24	Nonuser	155	2.36	.75
	User	276	2.46	.69
ITEM 25	Nonuser	161	2.29	.76
	User	277	2.44	.77
ITEM 26	Nonuser	158	2.29	.76
	User	275	2.50	.76
ITEM 27	Nonuser	160	2.60	.83
	User	272	2.84	.81
ITEM 28	Nonuser	140	2.40	.66
	User	260	2.35	.70
ITEM 29	Nonuser	156	2.82	.70
	User	276	3.07	.73
ITEM 30	Nonuser	161	3.19	.51
	User	283	3.15	.62
ITEM 31	Nonuser	157	2.62	.70
	User	277	2.64	.72

TABLE 19 (continued)

		Number of Cases	Mean	SD
ITEM 32	Nonuser	158	2.85	.72
	User	277	3.01	.66
ITEM 33	Nonuser	143	2.53	.74
	User	270	2.63	.75
ITEM 34	Nonuser	156	2.75	.73
	User	280	2.90	.67
ITEM 35	Nonuser	155	2.62	.77
	User	272	2.45	.72
ITEM 36	Nonuser	158	2.68	.66
	User	279	2.82	.65
ITEM 37	Nonuser	160	2.63	.77
	User	281	2.75	.70

TABLE 20. Means, Standard Deviations and Pearson r for Satisfaction with Library Services and Materials for Students Only

		n	Mean	SD	Item-total r
38)	Library service	451	4.86	1.89	.60
39)	Library materials for research	444	4.57	1.75	.57
40)	Library materials for teaching	406	4.66	1.75	.50
41)	Library materials for students	444	4.99	1.76	.62
42)	Book collection	444	4.80	1.80	.58
43)	Reserve materials	439	4.67	1.82	.58
44)	Staff help	446	4.81	2.34	.54
45)	Physical environment	447	4.48	1.98	.35

TABLE 21. Responses on Library Instruction by Faculty and Students

	Students		Faculty	
	n	%	n	%
Yes	348	(77%)	16	(76%)
No	40	(9%)	2	(10%)
Don't know	64	(14%)	3	(14%)
Total	452	(100%)	21	(100%)

TABLE 22. Desirable Library Changes by Faculty and Students

	Students	Faculty
No changes necessary	8	–
A new circulation system, with library cards	142	4
Open stacks, i.e., books stored in open shelves	85	3
Changes in the environment (e.g., lighting, heating, furniture, etc.)	122	5
Changes in the library hours	223	9
Other	24	11

Library hours are limited because of staff shortages, and the librarians seem to be aware of this problem. According to the students, the second most important change was a new circulation system with library cards; the faculty, however, wanted changes in the environment (lighting, heating, furniture, etc.). The third change requested was the establishment of open stacks. Only eight students indicated that no changes were necessary.

Respondents were asked to mark only one change. However, many questionnaires returned with more than one change checked. For this reason, the table indicates the number of respondents checking an item. No percentages are reported.

RECOMMENDATIONS

The development of an index of library use is recommended, combined with a sophisticated measure of frequency of use. A multi-dimensional measure of library use is also recommended, since this would take into consideration the multi-dimensional nature of library use. Moreover, since a need exists for further exploration and expansion of the attitude scales, more items should be included in order to allow a better understanding of the factors appearing in the attitude scales. The use of a different sampling procedure that would guarantee the representativeness of the sample, as far as academic class is concerned, is also suggested.

Library use surveys should be conducted within other departmental libraries to find out if the characteristics of the students are similar to those of the students in the English Department.

An investigation of the attitudes of students in other departments would be enlightening in supporting or disproving the findings in the English Department Library.

REFERENCE NOTES

1. Nancy Birk and Dimitris Karageorgiou, "Academic Libraries in Greece: A New Profile," *Libri* 38 (Number 2, 1988): 81-93; Nancy Birk, An Overview of Greek Libraries," *Ohio Media Spectrum* 39 (Winter 1987): 8.

2. Ibid.

3. Dean H. Keller, "A Report on Needs and Opportunities of the Central Library, Aristotle University, Thessaloniki, Greece, for Which Training, Education, and Support can be provided by the Kent State Universities Libraries, Kent, Ohio, U.S.A.," unpublished report, (1989); *The World of Learning* 11th ed. (London, England: Europa Publications Limited, 1990) p. 606; and *The College Blue Book: Tabular Data* (New York: Macmillan, 1989) p. 342.

4. Alex Noel-Tod, "Report on the Library of the Department of English Language and Literature, Aristotle University of Thessaloniki, Greece," unpublished report, (1989).

5. Leon Carnovsky, "Education for Librarianship Abroad: Greece," *Library Trends* 12 (October 1963): 158-165.

6. Richard Phillips Palmer, "Toward Improving Librarianship in Greece: Needs Assessment and Recommendations," unpublished report (1978).

7. Geoffrey Ford, *User Studies: An Introductory Guide and Select Bibliography* (Sheffield: University of Sheffield, Center for Research on User Studies, 1977), p. 4.

8. Edward W. Minium, *Statistical Reasoning in Psychology and Education*. (New York: John Wiley & Sons, 1970), p. 262.

9. Ibid., p. 263.

10. Ibid.

11. Thomas Michael Peischl, *A User Study of a University Library System: An Investigation of the Perceived Needs of a University Library's Patrons* (PhD Dissertation, University of Northern Colorado, 1979); *User Surveys* SPEC Kit, no. 148; *User Studies in ARL Libraries* SPEC Kit, no. 101; *User Surveys and Evaluation of Library Services* SPEC Kit, No. 71; *User Statistics and Studies* SPEC Kit, no. 25; *User Surveys* SPEC Flyer, No. 24, Washington, DC: Systems and Procedures Exchange Center, Association of Research Libraries).

Appendix 1

STUDENT QUESTIONNAIRE

Check the appropriate answer. Your answers will be considered confidential. Your cooperation will contribute towards making the library an effective partner in the educational process.

PART I

1) Sex:

    _____ Male _____ Female

2) Cumulative Grade Point Average:
    _____ (a) 8.50-10
    _____ (b) 7-8.49
    _____ (c) 5.5-6.99
    _____ (d) Below 5.49

3) Academic Class
    _____ (a) Fourth year
    _____ (b) Third year
    _____ (c) Second year
    _____ (d) First year

4) Was the English department your first choice for an academic career?

    _____ Yes _____ No

5) If you could choose again, would the English Department be your first choice?

    _____ Yes _____ No

6) What is the population of the city or town or village in which you grew up?
    _____ (a) 500,000 or more
    _____ (b) 100,000 to 499,999
    _____ (c) 50,000 to 99,999
    _____ (d) 12,000 to 49,999
    _____ (e) less than 12,000

7) Are you planning to go to work immediately after graduation?
_____ Yes _____ No

8) Are you planning to continue your studies through a second Bachelor's, Master's, or Ph.D. later on in your career?
_____ Yes _____ No

PART II

9) Last time you entered your departmental library, what was the primary reason for your visit? (MARK ANY THAT APPLY)
_____ (a) to study my own materials
_____ (b) to borrow library materials
_____ (c) to check the card catalog
_____ (d) to use the reserved books
_____ (e) to browse through the collection
_____ (f) to ask something from the librarian
_____ (g) Other. Specify _____.

10) How many times did you enter your departmental library last week?
_____ (a) None
_____ (b) 1 to 3
_____ (c) 4 to 9
_____ (d) 10 or more

11) Last week, how many times did you enter the library primarily to study your own materials?
_____ (a) None
_____ (b) 1 to 3
_____ (c) 4 to 9
_____ (d) 10 or more

12) Last week, how many times did you enter the library primarily to use library materials such as books, periodicals, reserve, etc.?
_____ (a) None
_____ (b) 1 to 3
_____ (c) 4 to 9
_____ (d) 10 or more

13) Last week, of the total number of times you entered the library, how many were to complete a specific assignment for a class?
   _____ (a) None
   _____ (b) 1 to 3
   _____ (c) 4 to 9
   _____ (d) 10 or more

14) If you did not enter the library last week, please indicate your reasons for not entering it?
   _____ (a) I didn't have time
   _____ (b) I didn't need it
   _____ (c) It was not open when I wanted to go
   _____ (d) It did not have the materials I wanted
   _____ (e) I found the books I need elsewhere
   _____ (f) Other. Specify _____.

15) Are you using other libraries apart from your departmental library?
   _____ Yes   _____ No

16) If yes, which other library or libraries are you using? (CHECK ALL THAT APPLY):
   _____ Central Library
   _____ British Council Library
   _____ American Center Library
   _____ Public Library. Specify _____.
   _____ Other. Specify _____.

PART III

Answer the following items by checking whether you SA = Strongly Agree, A = Agree, D = Disagree, SD = Strongly Disagree, N/A = Not Applicable.

	SA	A	D	SD	N/A
17) My professors and lecturers require that I use the library for specific assignments.	___	___	___	___	___

	SA	A	D	SD	N/A

18) The library provides
services that are
important to me as
an individual. ___ ___ ___ ___ ___

19) The items I want from
the library are always
available. ___ ___ ___ ___ ___

20) The books are easy
to locate. ___ ___ ___ ___ ___

21) The library is noisy. ___ ___ ___ ___ ___

22) The library of the
English Department
serves primarily faculty. ___ ___ ___ ___ ___

23) The library hours are
convenient. ___ ___ ___ ___ ___

24) The quality of my
departmental library's
collection is very good. ___ ___ ___ ___ ___

25) The size of my
departmental library's
collection adequately
meets my needs. ___ ___ ___ ___ ___

26) The library is a pleasant
place to visit. ___ ___ ___ ___ ___

27) Use of the library affects
the students' final grade. ___ ___ ___ ___ ___

	SA	A	D	SD	N/A
28) The library of the English Department is important primarily for teaching purposes.	___	___	___	___	___
29) Use of the library is important for the academic success of the students.	___	___	___	___	___
30) My professors and lecturers recommend the use of the library.	___	___	___	___	___
31) The library of the English Department serves primarily students.	___	___	___	___	___
32) The library of the English Department is important for both teaching and research.	___	___	___	___	___
33) The library of the English Department serves both faculty and students equally.	___	___	___	___	___
34) The library is too crowded.	___	___	___	___	___
35) The library of the English Department is important primarily for research purposes.	___	___	___	___	___
36) The library is clean and neat.	___	___	___	___	___

SA   A   D   SD   N/A

37) The library doesn't
    have enough places
    to sit.   ____ ____ ____ ____ ____

Circle the number that most closely describes your degree of satisfaction or dissatisfaction with the following:

38) Library service
    Very Satisfied 1 2 3 4 5 6 7 8 Very dissatisfied

39) Library materials for research
    Very Satisfied 1 2 3 4 5 6 7 8 Very dissatisfied

40) Library materials for teaching
    Very Satisfied 1 2 3 4 5 6 7 8 Very dissatisfied

41) Library materials for students
    Very Satisfied 1 2 3 4 5 6 7 8 Very dissatisfied

42) Book collection
    Very Satisfied 1 2 3 4 5 6 7 8 Very dissatisfied

43) Reserve Materials
    Very Satisfied 1 2 3 4 5 6 7 8 Very dissatisfied

44) Staff help
    Very Satisfied 1 2 3 4 5 6 7 8 Very dissatisfied

45) Physical environment
    Very Satisfied 1 2 3 4 5 6 7 8 Very dissatisfied

46) Would you like to see a formal course on how to use the
    library offered to the students?
    _____ YES _____ NO _____ DON'T KNOW

47) Which one of the following changes would most increase your
     satisfaction with the library (CHECK ONE):
     _____ (a) No changes necessary
     _____ (b) a new circulation system, with library cards
     _____ (c) open stacks, i.e., books stored in open shelves
     _____ (d) changes in the environment (e.g., lighting,
                 heating, furniture, etc.)
     _____ (e) changes in the library hours
     _____ (f) Other. Specify _____.

The investigator would be interested in any comments you care to
make about the library's conditions. Please use the back page.
Thank you for your cooperation.

Appendix 2

FACULTY QUESTIONNAIRE

Check the appropriate answer. Your answers will be considered confidential.

PART I

1) Sex:
   _____ Male   _____ Female

2) Highest Academic Degree:
   _____ (a) Bachelor's
   _____ (b) Master's
   _____ (c) Ph.D.

3) Faculty Rank:
   _____ (a) Graduate (EMY)
   _____ (b) Assistants working on a Ph.D.
   _____ (c) EEP teachers
   _____ (d) Lecturer
   _____ (e) Asssistant Professor
   _____ (f) Associate Professor
   _____ (g) Professor

4) Length of service in the English Department of the Aristotle University:
   _____ (a) 1-2 years
   _____ (b) 3-5 years
   _____ (c) 6-9 years
   _____ (d) 10+ years

PART II

5) Last time you entered your departmental library, what was the primary reason? (MARK ANY THAT APPLY)
   _____ (a) to study my own materials
   _____ (b) to borrow library materials
   _____ (c) to check the card catalog

_____ (d) to use the reserved books
_____ (e) to browse through the collection
_____ (f) to ask something from the librarian
_____ (g) Other. Specify _____.

6) How many times did you enter your departmental library last week?
_____ (a) None
_____ (b) 1 to 3
_____ (c) 4 to 9
_____ (d) 10 or more

7) Last week, how many times did you enter the library primarily to study your <u>own</u> materials?
_____ (a) None
_____ (b) 1 to 3
_____ (c) 4 to 9
_____ (d) 10 or more

8) Last week, how many times did you enter the library primarily to use <u>library</u> materials such as books, periodicals, reserve, etc.?
_____ (a) None
_____ (b) 1 to 3
_____ (c) 4 to 9
_____ (d) 10 or more

9) If you did not enter the library last week, please indicate your reasons for not entering it?
_____ (a) I didn't have time
_____ (b) I didn't need it
_____ (c) It was not open when I wanted to go
_____ (d) It did not have the materials I wanted
_____ (e) I found the books I need elsewhere
_____ (f) Other. Specify _____.

10) Do you prefer to use materials:
_____ (a) in your office
_____ (b) in the library
_____ (c) in your home
_____ (d) Other. Specify _____.

11) Are you using other libraries apart from your departmental library?

_____ Yes   _____ No

12) If yes, which other library or libraries are you using? (CHECK ALL THAT APPLY):

_____ Central Library
_____ British Council Library
_____ American Center Library
_____ Public Library. Specify _____.
_____ Other. Specify _____.

PART III

Answer the following items by checking whether you SA = Strongly Agree, A = Agree, D = Disagree, SD = Strongly Disagree, N/A = Not Applicable.

	SA	A	D	SD	N/A
13) I require that the students use the library for specific assignments.	___	___	___	___	___
14) It provides services that are important to me as an individual.	___	___	___	___	___
15) The items I want from the library are always available.	___	___	___	___	___
16) The books are easy to locate.	___	___	___	___	___
17) The library is noisy.	___	___	___	___	___
18) The library of the English Department serves primarily students.	___	___	___	___	___

	SA	A	D	SD	N/A
19) The library hours are convenient.	___	___	___	___	___
20) The quality of my departmental library's collection is very good.	___	___	___	___	___
21) The size of my departmental library's collection adequately meets my needs.	___	___	___	___	___
22) The library is a pleasant place to visit.	___	___	___	___	___
23) Use of the library affects the students' final grade.	___	___	___	___	___
24) The library of the English Department is important primarily for teaching purposes.	___	___	___	___	___
25) Use of the library is important for the academic success of the students.	___	___	___	___	___
26) I recommend the use of the library.	___	___	___	___	___
27) The library of the English Department serves primarily faculty.	___	___	___	___	___
28) The library of the English Department is important for both teaching and research.	___	___	___	___	___

SA   A   D   SD   N/A

29) The library of the
English Department
serves both faculty
and students equally.   ___ ___ ___ ___ ___

30) The library is too
crowded.   ___ ___ ___ ___ ___

31) The library of the
English Department is
important primarily for
research purposes.   ___ ___ ___ ___ ___

32) The library is clean
and neat.   ___ ___ ___ ___ ___

33) The library doesn't have
enough places to sit.   ___ ___ ___ ___ ___

Circle the number that most closely describes your degree of satisfaction or dissatisfaction with the following:

34) Library service
Very Satisfied 1 2 3 4 5 6 7 8 Very dissatisfied

35) Library materials for research
Very Satisfied 1 2 3 4 5 6 7 8 Very dissatisfied

36) Library materials for teaching
Very Satisfied 1 2 3 4 5 6 7 8 Very dissatisfied

37) Library materials for students
Very Satisfied 1 2 3 4 5 6 7 8 Very dissatisfied

38) Book collection
Very Satisfied 1 2 3 4 5 6 7 8 Very dissatisfied

39) Reserve Materials
Very Satisfied 1 2 3 4 5 6 7 8 Very dissatisfied

40) Staff help
Very Satisfied 1 2 3 4 5 6 7 8 Very dissatisfied

41) Physical environment
Very Satisfied 1 2 3 4 5 6 7 8 Very dissatisfied

42) Would you like to see a formal course on how to use the library offered to the students?
_____ YES _____ NO _____ DON'T KNOW

43) Which one of the following changes would most increase your satisfaction with the library (CHECK ONE):
_____ (a) No changes necessary
_____ (b) a new circulation system, with library cards
_____ (c) open stacks, i.e., books stored in open shelves
_____ (d) changes in the environment (e.g., lighting, heating, furniture, etc.)
_____ (e) changes in the library hours
_____ (f) Other. Specify _____

The investigator would be interested in any comments you care to make about the library's conditions. Please use the back page. Thank you for your cooperation.

Kent State University, Kent, Ohio, and Aristotle University, Thessaloniki, Greece: An Exchange Program

Thomas M. Davis

Thessaloniki, a city of some 900,000, is situated at the head of the Thermaic Gulf in northern Greece. On most days, Mt. Olympus, some 90 kilometers to the southwest, is clearly visible. The city is quite a cosmopolitan one, reflecting the influences not only of Greece but also of the Balkans and Turkey; it is essentially a cross-roads of cultures. During the two years (1982-84) I spent at Aristotle University as Fulbright Professor of American Literature, I came to know and appreciate the cultural diversity of the city and the university. Aristotle has about 60,000 students, and the variety of the students and their backgrounds was reflected in my classes in American Literature.

After the first year, I asked my colleagues what they thought about establishing an exchange program with Kent State University. Kent professors could have the different experience of teaching in Thessaloniki; Aristotle professors could benefit by reduced teaching loads and a chance to spend a year doing research in Kent's very good library. We were able, by the fall of 1984, to conclude a general agreement between the two universities providing for the direct cooperation between faculties, colleges, and departments of the two schools. The terms of the agreement were purposely kept general; once annexes defining specific details between departments were agreed upon, they then became part of the general agreement. The Rector of Aristotle University, Dimitrios Fatouros, came to Kent State in the fall of 1984 to sign the agreement; to

197

extend it into the second triennium, President Michael Schwartz went to Thessaloniki in the spring of 1988.

The cooperation began with the direct exchange of faculty in areas covered by the annexes. As of the fall of 1990, 17 faculty members from Kent have taught in the English Department at Aristotle or assisted in the work of the English Department Library and Central Library. Eight faculty members from Aristotle have been in residence at Kent State: three professors of linguistics, three lecturers in linguistics, and one person each in chemistry and education. During this same period, a number of students have been appointed as graduate assistants or teaching fellows at Kent. These students were in music, history, English, library science, and political science. To date, 16 students have received the MA or MLS, and several are in doctoral programs here or at other universities.

Quite early in the exchange, we became aware of the need for basic work in various departmental libraries and at the Central Library at Aristotle. We decided on a program that would address as effectively as possible the complex problems of Aristotle's library system. Insofar as we could determine, there were about 65 libraries; most were departmental ones, but the size ranged from several hundred volumes to several thousand. The systems of cataloging these books varied from collection to collection. Some were entered in the Central Library catalog; many–perhaps most–were not. Some of these collections were supervised by relatively well-trained personnel; others had no supervision at all. (I might note here that except for the practical programs in the Technological Education Institutes, which have a three-year program in library science and a six month's practicum, there is no bachelor's program in library science in Greece, nor are there any graduate studies.)

Working with our colleagues in Thessaloniki, we decided on a three-part program to address their needs. First, we would send staff to accomplish certain specific projects. Second, in our School of Library Science, we would train as many students for the MLS as we could obtain funding for. And, finally, for those students from the Technological Education Institute (TEI), particularly those who were already working in Aristotle's Central Library or departmental libraries, we would provide a six- to nine-month advanced training program in our central library.

We began our work in the Department of English Library. The Library is in a fenced-off area in a large reading room. Books do not circulate (except to faculty), and students do most of their reading/ research in this limited facility. The holdings, as might be expected, were unpredictable, reflecting the areas of individual faculties' interests rather than a systematic and organized approach. During the first year I was there, there was no librarian at all; individual faculty members took turns keeping the library open, resulting often in very limited hours. The catalog list of books was not current, and sections were often in a quite confused state.

In addition to the English Department library, there was an American Center Library, under the aegis of the U.S. Information Service (USIS). This library was extensively used by my students. It is essentially like a small American library, with trained personnel and a fairly good selection of books in American literature. Yet here, too, the materials available were limited. Since the USIS libraries try to have representative holdings in a number of areas of potential interest to their clientele, it is not possible to allocate their funds primarily in one or two areas.

To address the problems in the Department of English library, we sent our Associate Curator of Rare Books, Nancy Birk, to reorganize the material there. The books–some 25,000, listed by Dewey decimal, Library of Congress (LC), and sometimes according to order number–were all removed from the shelves. There was no catalog that presented an accurate list of the holdings of the library. So Birk began at the beginning and created a comprehensive catalog, including all books under LC numbers. She also examined the book orders of the department, checking to see that holdings needed filling out and–given the limited resources–to make sure of their adequacy. She spent some time doing research on the holdings of other libraries in Greece, visiting most of them. Birk's work at Aristotle, after a full year, was about two-thirds completed. The following year, we sent a second librarian to complete the work.

At this time, we also made arrangements with the U.S. Education Service in Greece to obtain special Fulbright funding for one scholarship at Kent for three terms of work toward the Master's of Library Science degree. After the three terms of formal course work were finished, students were assigned to a six-month practicum in our Central Library, which was developed by our Associate Dean of Libraries, Dean Keller. Working in the Central Library of Kent State University, these graduates received additional experience in various stages of library operation.

Finally, for staff members of the Central Library in Thessaloniki or of departmental libraries who did not have a Bachelor's degree, or who possessed the certificate from the TEI, a flexible program at Kent of from six to nine months was developed, one that could be adapted to the needs of each individual. Participants were given practical experience in a wide variety of library technologies: acquisitions, serials. bibliographic control, cataloging and processing, reference, and circulation. All classes in the School of Library and Information Science were also open to these individuals, and visits to other libraries in the area were arranged.

Finally, we began our work in the Central Library. During the next three terms, Evelina Smith, the library director of one of Kent's regional campus libraries, went to the Central Library to initiate the work there. Smith spent some time determining the basic organization and staff needs, and made a series of recommendations that would improve the effectiveness of the library's operation. One of the central problems she addressed was the number of staff members in the library who–except for the TEI graduates–had no practical or professional library training. Smith noted in her recommendations that equivalent-sized libraries with a book collection of one million volumes ordinarily have working staffs of over 100 people. Yet the Central Library, with more than a million volumes, had a staff of only 22 people and three TEI practicum students. Smith noted that the only way the Central Library could hope to stay abreast of present advances in library services was by hiring additional staff and by library automation.

Smith then wrote a proposal and prepared a budget, and presented these to the Rector of the university, emphasizing the advantages for the university if it became part of on-line Online Computer Library Center (OCLC)-Europe. The money was allocated for that program, and she began training staff in the library, particularly the TEI students and one staff member with computer experience, to prepare them for the anticipated installation of OCLC. In addition, she made specific recommendations for increases in staff–professionally trained librarians as supervisors in the Circulation Department, the Reference Department, the Cataloguing Department, and the Acquisitions Department. In her recommendations and discussions with the rector and the director of the Library, she stressed the need for long-range planning and the careful allocation of resources to provide the professionally trained staff that the Central Library needed.

At this point, in the spring of 1989, with the reorganization of the English Department Library complete and work beginning in the Central Library, it was decided that Dean Keller, the Associate Dean of Kent State University's Libraries, should spend a term in Thessaloniki with the intention of making recommendations to the administration at Aristotle University about the needs of the Central Library and of the library system generally. We were also at a point where we needed to decide what would be our best approach to continue work in the Central Library: to shift to departmental libraries or to try to continue assisting in both areas.

Professor Keller submitted to Rector Trakatellis an extensive report indicating the basic and immediate needs of the Central Library. The most pressing need, he noted, was for the addition of professionally trained staff, and he recommended at the very least a minimum of two additional staff members. One of these, he suggested, should be assigned as head of a reorganized reference department; the second should serve as liaison with the various departmental libraries. His second major recommendation addressed the establishment of an administrative structure in the Central Library. There was no one in the Central Library in a supervisory position except the Director. Professor Keller recommended that departments should be defined and supervisors appointed for each. And he recommended periodic evaluations of the staff and supervisors.

After his survey of the general needs of the Central Library, Professor Keller indicated that reference service was perhaps the single most underdeveloped area. He recommended, as I have noted, that a staff member with professional training be appointed to head the reference service. Finally, he recommended that the departmental libraries, which were funded by individual academic departments with no official connection to the Central Library, be administered by the Central Library. In this context, he suggested that the rector would have to make this a requirement and that a new staff member would need to be provided to coordinate the process. One responsibility of the new staff member would be to create a union catalog of all library holdings, as well as to conduct a survey of all departmental libraries.

Professor Keller also interviewed the seven TEI students who were then taking their practicum experience in the Central Library. Since TEI students receive the only practical library training available in Greece, he recommended that efforts be undertaken to strengthen the practicum program and to provide a coordinator to oversee it. Kent Faculty have found the TEI students very conscientious and hard-working. Four have come to Kent to work in our practical training program, and we are attempting to find funding to increase that number.

To oversee the installation of OCLC-Europe and to train Central Library staff in the use of computers, Kent's automation specialist, Michael Kreyche, went to Thessaloniki for the fall of 1989. He was also concerned with working with the staff in the Central Library to introduce the use of the OCLC system for cataloging and interlibrary loan. The one person there trained in computer use, Paschalis Raptis, had accepted a Fulbright scholarship to come to Kent to work on his MLS. Before he left for Kent, he introduced Professor Kreyche to the system there, and noted the existing problems. Kreyche also worked with various departmental libraries and proposed adapting the basic cataloging system that had been developed by the Central Library to departmental libraries as well. The single IBM computer on campus was already operating at close to its capacity, and there was no access to it from the Central Library. Yet, the basic cataloging system would work for departmental libraries.

Kreyche's work began to center on the Physics Department Library, which had already begun under the supervision of a full-time librarian to consolidate the department's many collections into a single library. This library was located in the same building as the IBM, and a terminal was easily installed. The software was already available, since the librarian hired had worked in the library in Crete, where the software had been developed (the librarian's husband, a computer scientist, had set up an IBM system at the University of Crete). Kreyche recommended to the Physics Library Committee that they use the software from Crete. The Committee agreed and took the initiative to make the necessary arrangements. After Kreyche had returned to Kent, he was informed that the software had been installed at Thessaloniki and had been successfully demonstrated.

Professor Kreyche also visited the library at the University of Crete and met with Michael Tzekakis, the director of the Library. Given the compatibility of the software, they discussed the possibility of further cooperation between the two universities, since the library automation program at the University of Crete is the most successful one in Greece. By evaluating and familiarizing himself with the system in Crete, Professor Kreyche was able to include in his recommendations specific details for sharing technology with the University of Crete and for the development of an adequate computer system in Thessaloniki (also indicating the stages necessary for its development). As did Professor Keller, Professor Kreyche emphasized the need for additional staff, particularly in developing a reference service, but in other areas as well. And he provided detailed recommendations addressing the further needs of the Central Library in developing an adequate automation system.

At the end of this process, after Professor Kreyche's return to Kent, Dr. Don L. Tolliver, Kent's Dean of Libraries and Media Services, visited Thessaloniki and the University of Crete to consult with the directors of the libraries and to meet with the rector at Thessaloniki to determine what kind of future support would be available and to see in what way the university had responded to the various recommendations presented by both Associate Dean Keller and Professor Kreyche. Dr. Tolliver also recommended that the University of Thessaloniki consider a more formal arrangement with the libraries of the University of Crete. He noted that the initial program established in the Physics Department indicated what could be achieved by such an arrangement. His visit to the University of Crete had convinced him of the high quality and modern automation of the system that was being developed there. He also presented an address at the American Center on the state of library automation, and gave a talk with a long period of discussion at the TEI.

Greek libraries share many of the same problems: administrative support is not always evident; inadequate budgets result in inadequate collection; in too many places, the library is understaffed; and the basic funds for automation so necessary to the future of a modern library are not always available. The problems in the Central Library in Thessaloniki, however, are exacerbated by the fact that it is simply stumbling to catch up. More administrative support is necessary, more staff is urgently needed, and funds must be made available for purchasing the necessary technology that can make the Central Library into the kind of service to students and faculty that it must become. Until some hard and firm decisions are made by the university administration, the future for the library system there does not look very promising. On the other hand, we have found that Kent State University faculty have the expertise to address some of the major problems and that the practicum arranged in Kent's Central Library, as well as the work in the School of Library and Information Science, does respond to basic needs in Aristotle's library system. What we are always aware of in the exchange process, however, is that our system is not theirs and that a library system so differently organized from ours will not be able to make the changes needed without some false starts and without major difficulties. Our contribution to the exchange is to help in whatever ways we can, as we are asked.

A Greek Librarian in America: Personal Reflections on an Eight-Month Practicum at the Kent State University Libraries

Athena Salaba

INTRODUCTION

Library Science is taught in Greece at the Technological Education tion Institute (TEI) as a department of the School of Administration and Economics. There are two such schools in Greece, one in Athens (established in 1977) and the other in Thessaloniki (Salonika) (established in 1981). The program is made up of six semesters of coursework and a seventh practicum semester in a library. I did part of my practicum in the Public Library of Kavala and the rest of it in the Central Library of the Aristotle University in Thessaloniki. Upon graduation, in June 1986, I attended a six-month seminar on computers and programming in the Greek Organization of Production (EL.KE.PA.).

While I was a student, I worked at the Central Library of the Aristotle University of Thessaloniki for ten months on a special project. This project involved organizing an exhibition of library materials on Thessaloniki, commemorating the 2300 years since the establishment of the city. On October 5, 1986, I started working in the Central Library on a regular appointment, after an opening for six positions for librarians became available. My position is a contract-based position. Since then, I have worked mainly as a cataloger in the Technical Services Department.

There have been a number of opportunities for attending seminars as an employee of the Library. Two such seminars I attended

205

were "Information and Technology in Libraries," offered by the EL. KE. PA., and "Cataloging," offered by the Institute of Continuing Education (IDE), which was available to employees in the public sector of the economy.

EXCHANGE PROGRAM

The Kent State University Libraries offer a nine-month training program to Greek librarians from the Aristotle University through an exchange program between it and Kent State University. The program involves instruction, training, and practical experience in the different departments in the library, and it is adapted to meet the needs and interests of the visiting librarians. The program includes: General Orientation to the Campus and to the Library, Acquisitions, Serials, Bibliographic Control, Cataloging and Processing, Reference, and Circulation.

In addition to training on-site at the library, the exchange librarians can attend non-credit courses in Kent State University's School of Library and Information Science and can also visit other libraries (academic, public, and special). In this program, I had the opportunity to visit the Kent State University Libraries for eight months, from January 19 to September 20, 1990.

My interest is basically concentrated in technical services. However, I wanted my experience in American libraries to be well-rounded and to include some familiarity with operations in all the other departments and services of the library. So, with the assistance of the Kent State University Library librarians who were responsible for the exchange program and who had already been at the libraries of the Aristotle University under the same exchange program and knew the needs of the libraries there, I made an outline of my eight-month stay at the Kent Libraries, listed the different departments in which I wanted to work, and determined how long I should spend in each department.

First of all, I had a tour of the Main Library to acquire a general idea about the several departments and services there. I attended a meeting of the Library Services Council, which consists of the Dean of the Libraries and Media Service; the Associate Dean; the Director of Library Services (who is the chair of the council); the

Assistant to the Dean; the Budget Officer; the heads of the Reference, Circulation, Acquisitions/Serials, Cataloging Departments, Special Collections and Branch libraries; and the Systems Analyst. This meeting takes place about every fifteen days, and its subject is library operation.

TECHNICAL SERVICES TRAINING

Bibliographic Control Unit

I started working first in the Bibliographic Control Unit (BCU), a division in Technical Services. This unit works both on the library's on-line catalog named CATALYST (a NOTIS system) and on On-line Computer Library Center (OCLC). There, I learned to check the order slips in CATALYST for duplicates. If there is no record, the process involves checking OCLC and transferring the appropriate record into CATALYST. In addition to this, records that are found in OCLC are edited and input into OCLC and CATALYST. I worked for two-and-a-half months at BCU, becoming familiar and competent in dealing with an on-line system. I had had some previous experience with OCLC functions, because the Central Library of the Aristotle University has been a member of OCLC since October 1989. The most important skill I acquired while working in the BCU was how to catalog in an on-line environment using Machine Readable Cataloging (MARC) format for the records.

Cataloging

I moved next to the Cataloging department. Under the supervision of a professional librarian, I worked on checking non-Library of Congress (LC) records from OCLC records and on original cataloging for material lacking OCLC records. In this way, I gained additional experience in cataloging material according to Anglo-American Cataloging Rules, second edition, revised (AACR2 Rev.), creating subject headings according to the Library of Congress Subject Headings, and classifying material according to the Library of Congress Classification System. Because original cataloging involves authority work, I learned about the philosophy of authority work and I worked on authorities, checking the authority files and creating authority records. Authority work is not highly developed in Greek libraries; although some libraries have authority files, this work is done manually in card-catalog format and not in an on-line environment. Working in this area, I learned the whole operation of authorities and the MARC authority format.

Special Collections

After spending one month in the Cataloging Department, I moved to Special Collections. That department consists of two sections: Rare Books and Archives. In the Rare Books section are collections that the library and the university are interested in. The collection is strong in English, especially American literature, American theater, and Indians of North America. Mostly, I worked on cataloging rare books from several collections, such as the Queen Collection of Western Americana and three collections of detective fiction and true crime. The collections were in the Robert Hayman library, the Albert Borowitz library, and some material located in the general collection of the department. For the occasion of a major exhibition of the Borowitz Collection, the Special Collections staff had to organize and publish a catalog. For this catalog, material that would be used had to be described, photographs were taken, and captions were written. I participated in this project.

Reference

Every librarian should experience the reference department. It is a basic department that shows how all the different functions in a library can work together to support the information needs of the library user. I spent two weeks in Reference observing the Reference desk, where patrons seek all kinds of information from the reference librarians. I learned how to search in the CD-ROMs for a specific subject, observed the whole process followed in an on-line search in Dialog, and worked on a project to find which new editions of reference materials had been purchased for the Library.

Interlibrary Loan, Circulation, and Acquisitions

While I did not actually work in other departments, I spent some time observing other library services and activities. Those services were Interlibrary Loan, Circulation, and Acquisitions. In Interlibrary Loan, I saw the process of lending material to other libraries and borrowing material from other libraries using the OCLC interlibrary loan subsystem. In addition to that, I saw the statistics that were kept for interlibrary loan and I saw how the library's policy for interlibrary loan was interpreted. In Circulation, after I studied the operation manual for the Circulation Department, I went through the processes of circulating the material, billing the customers, sorting returned materials, and placing materials on reserve for courses offered at the university. In the Acquisitions and Serials Department, I learned how the materials budget is allocated to the different schools and departments of the university, and what percentage of the budget is for periodicals and what percentage is for monographs. I followed the process of ordering material from U.S. and foreign vendors and of checking material prices. I learned how to work with approval plans, observed the process of receiving material, and saw what was necessary in the preparation of the library's statistical reports.

ATTENDING CLASSES

As already mentioned, I could attend some classes in the School of Library and Information Science. In the Spring semester, I audited three courses: Organization of Library Material, Advanced Cataloging, and Rare Books. In the first course, Organization of Library Material, I was taught to catalog books according to the AACR2 1988 Revised Edition; keep authority files; classify according to the Library of Congress Classification System and the Dewey Decimal Classification; and create subject headings according to the Sears List of Subject Headings and Library of Congress Subject Headings. Advanced Cataloging dealt with on-line cataloging, OCLC applications, and use of the OCLC MARC Format for non-book material. The Rare Book course was concerned with the organizing of a special collection, the acquiring of rare books, and cataloging them. In the summer, I attended two workshops given by the School of Library and Information Science. The first workshop was "Automating the Library," where the students were taught to write a request for proposal, what the needs for a library automated system are, what the library should ask of the vendor, and how the library should negotiate a contract with the vendor. The second workshop I attended was "On-line Reference." In that workshop, I learned how to search on-line in databases such as Dialog and Bibliographical Retrieval Service (BRS). I had training in the content and format of on-line databases, so we could search on-line on a specific subject. Each workshop lasted five days.

VISITING LIBRARIES

The third part of my program at the Kent State University Libraries was the opportunity to visit other libraries. I started out with the branch libraries on the Kent State University's main campus. Visited first was the Chemistry/Physics Library, a library that has material (mostly periodicals) intended in large part for use by graduate students and faculty. The next branch library visited was the Map Library in the Department of Geography. This is a special library with a collection made up mainly of atlases and maps. The Architecture Branch Library and the Music Library, each specialized in its field, were the last two visited.

In addition to the main and branch libraries on the main campus at Kent State University, there are libraries on the university's seven regional campuses. I visited two of the regional libraries, the Trumbull Campus Library and the Stark Campus Library. As a result of these visits, it was possible for me to gain an understanding of the intricacies of a comprehensive library system that consists of a main library, the branch libraries, and regional libraries. I was also able to observe how these libraries cooperate with the main library and how the system maintains an on-line union catalog.

Besides the Kent State University Libraries, I visited several other academic and public libraries in Ohio. The academic libraries visited were: the Ohio State University Library; Akron University's Main Library and its Science Library; the Library of Hiram College; the Case Western Reserve University Library; and the Classics Library of the University of Cincinnati. The Cleveland Public Library and the Akron-Summit County Public Library were the public libraries visited. A visit was made also to the special library of the Cleveland Natural History Museum.

By participating in the program of the School of Library and Information Science, I was able to take advantage of field trips to still other libraries and library systems. On a trip to Washington DC, there was an opportunity to have a guided tour in the Library of the National Geographic Society, the Library of Congress, the Library of the Special Library Association, the Government Printing Office, and the National Archives. Another trip was made to OCLC in Columbus, where a tour was given of all the OCLC departments. During this tour, retrospective conversion was described, as were such current projects as the development of Dewey Decimal Classification system.

SEMINARS AND MEETINGS

The state-supported academic libraries in Ohio have started working on a plan for an on-line library network system called OHIOLINK. In February, vendors who had responded to the Request for Proposal for OHIOLINK gave demonstrations of their programs for library administrators involved in the OHIOLINK project. The demonstrations took place in Columbus. Each week, for four weeks, two vendors demonstrated the various functions of their automated library system, such as Cataloging, Acquisitions and Serials, Collection Management, Circulation, and On-line Public Access Catalogs (OPACs). I had the great opportunity to attend all of the sessions.

A librarian always needs further training in new techniques of librarianship. During my stay at Kent, several seminars were organized, each of them on a particular subject. One was held at OCLC and was about descriptive cataloging based on the 1988 revised edition of AACR2. Lectures were given about the differences of the new-edition rules and how to solve some common and uncommon problems while cataloging books and non-book materials. At the end of the seminar, specific problems and questions were answered in a panel discussion.

THE NEED FOR AN EXCHANGE PROGRAM FOR GREEK LIBRARIES AND LIBRARIANS

The Library system at Aristotle University consists of the Central Library and about 90 branch libraries in the various departments and schools of the University. The Central Library does not have a current collection. All materials are for the branch libraries. Acquisitions are the branch libraries' responsibility. The Central Library receives the material and processes it. Cataloging, card production, inputting into the database, and labeling is the Central Library's responsibility.

In 1986, the Central Library started automating its functions. At this time, it has a network with a minicomputer, and the program holds a simple bibliographic record of the material. The program was developed in-house, and the records are not based on the MARC format. The University of Crete has developed a program for their libraries called *Ptolemeos*. The records are based on United States Machine Readable Cataloging (USMARC) requirements, and the modes that the program has are now cataloging and circulation. This program was installed at Aristotle University, but no MARC records exist as yet for Aristotle University materials. Hence, retrospective conversion has to be done so that the records can be loaded into the new system. Only materials acquired before 1986 are in the card catalog. After 1986, materials appear in both the card catalog and in the database. The information elements contained in the records are author, title, imprint, accession numbers, standard numbers (LCCN, ISBN, ISSN), and two subject headings. In 1989, the library at Aristotle University was connected with OCLC Europe, and cards and tapes with MARC records are provided for material found in the OCLC database. The card catalog consists of two parts: The foreign-language materials, where cataloging is done in English (with English subject headings), and the Greek-language material (with Greek subject headings).

No authority file exists in the library, and that is something that is needed. What is also needed is a bilingual authority control system.

That requires a very good authority file that will handle bilingual headings, since Library of Congress Subject Headings (LCSH) are used for the foreign-language materials and a Greek translation of the LCSH is used for Greek material.

A department similar to the Technical Services Department at the Kent State University Library is needed at Aristotle University. Creation of the Greek MARC format based on the USMARC format, authority, and bibliographic (with special consideration given to the needs of the Greek libraries) should likewise receive attention.

A project for retrospective conversion of the already existing catalog should be planned so that the library can have a union OPAC for the whole library system, the Central Library, and the branches. At the same time, new materials have to be cataloged in the MARC format. Since no one in the Central Library knows the MARC format, seminars should be given to the catalogers and others on the library's staff. Seminars for the branch librarians are likewise needed. Another department that is not well organized is the Reference Department. The Reference Department is housed in the Central Library, but it needs further development and a staff that knows how to run such a department.

The Central Library and some of the branch libraries have many rare books in their collections that are not treated as rare books and rare materials. A Special Collections department should be developed and the rare material should be housed in this department. Special cataloging has to be done for this material.

For all of these reasons, the Library at Aristotle University needs to increase its number of trained personnel. That will be possible with continued participation in exchange programs with well-organized libraries. Since many libraries in Greece lack librarians or well-trained staff library, staff should be encouraged to participate in such programs. Finally, library automation is something fairly new in Greece, but many libraries have started to automate themselves. To do this more successfully, an increase in the number of trained librarians is essential. Programs, such as the one I participated in at Kent State University, can help bring this about.

Index

Page references in italics indicate figures; t indicates table

School of Industrial Studies
(Thessaloniki), 12t
Schwartz, Michael, 198
Secondary education in Greece,
24
Services. *See* Library services
Smith, Evelina, 56,200
Special Collections
Aristotle University of
Thessaloniki, 213
Kent State University, 208
Stack capacity, Aristotle University
of Thessaloniki Department
of English, 131-132
Students
Aristotle University of
Thessaloniki, 152
Aristotle University of
Thessaloniki Department of
English
attitudes toward library,
169-177,171t-172t,173t,174t,
176t-177t,178t,179t,180t
circulation policies, 147-148,
153
data needed for survey, 158
enrollment, 157
frequency of library use,
164-166,165t,166t
library instruction, 181t
questionnaire, 184-190
reasons for library use, 163t,
163-164,164t
sample, 159-161,160t-161t
users versus nonusers,
166-169,167t-168t
Greek universities
access to library materials,
15,25,84
numbers, 12t
Kent State-University of
Thessaloniki cooperative
program, 197-204
preference for higher education
admission, 43-44,44t

Subscriptions. *See* Periodicals
Survey. *See* Users and user survey

Tavernaraki, Janet, 58
Teaching as library function,
170-174
Teaching methods
universities in Greece, 121
University of Crete, 112
Teaching staff. *See* Faculty
Technological Education Institutes.
See TEI
TEI (Technological Education
Institutes)
curriculum, 45-46,52-53
entrance examinations, 43-45
establishment, 42
faculty, 46-47
Kent State cooperative program,
197-204
library program, 205
TEI of Athens, Department of
Library Science
curriculum, 45-46
faculty, 46-48
positive and negative aspects,
48-50
TEI of Thessaloniki, Department of
Librarianship
curriculum, 45-46
faculty, 46-48
positive and negative aspects,
48-50
student preference for admission,
44t
Telecommunications. *See also*
Online Computer Library
Center; Online databases
Textbooks, University of Crete, 114
Thatcher government, 5
Thesaurus, 123
Time concepts, 121
Tolliver, Don L., 203
Training. *See* Library education;
Library instruction

Printed in the United States
by Baker & Taylor Publisher Services